# CUT AND FOLD
# TECHNIQUES FOR
# POP-UP DESIGNS

Paul Jackson

Laurence King Publishing

**LAURENCE KING**

Published in 2014 by
Laurence King Publishing Ltd
361–373 City Road
London EC1V 1LR
United Kingdom

Reprinted 2014, 2016, 2017, 2018

email: enquiries@laurenceking.com
www.laurenceking.com
© 2014 Paul Jackson

A catalogue record for this book is
available from the British Library.

ISBN: 978 1 78067 327 1

Designed by Struktur Design
Photography by Meidad Sochovolski
Senior editor: Peter Jones
Printed in China

# CUT AND FOLD TECHNIQUES FOR POP-UP DESIGNS

Paul Jackson

Laurence King Publishing

# Contents

We all love pop-ups! Their delightful blend of ingenuity and magic appeals to everyone, everywhere.

This unique book shows how to create simple cut-and-fold one-piece pop-ups that can be used as a ground for surface graphics, transforming conventional two-dimensional printing into attention-grabbing three-dimensional objects to be displayed and admired. Never again will your flyers, brochures, greetings cards, information leaflets, party invitations and even your CV look like junk mail, when presented in the third dimension.

Traditionally, one-piece pop-ups are intricately cut and folded to create sculptures of great complexity. However, the intricacy of these constructions breaks the card into many small facets and makes them unsuitable as a ground for readable text or big images. By contrast, this book introduces many unconventional pop-up techniques which still open a sheet of card into three-dimensions, but which enable the card to keep available many large, flat areas suitable for printing. These techniques for simplifying the surface also mean that pop-ups become much easier to design than their intricate sculptural predecessors. Even the simplest pop-up form made by the most inexperienced beginner can look impressive when surface graphics are added.

The book will also be of interest to people whose primary interest is three-dimensional form, rather than the printed surface. The unconventional pop-up techniques presented in the book will appeal to any designer interested in methods to create 3-D structures from 2-D sheet materials, including architects, textile designers, fashion designers and set designers. In this sense, perhaps the term 'pop-up' should be replaced with the term, 'cut-and-fold collapsible structure', which is less snappy, but more descriptive and serious-sounding.

This book is not a collection of formulaic templates to which surface graphics can be added, but a compendium of inspirational techniques that you can adapt and combine to create your own pop-up designs, each best suited to the specific needs of a design brief. This is an inspirational book, not a catalogue.

Everything in the book can be designed using basic graphic software and printed using a standard computer printer. For longer production runs, the surface graphics can be offset printed and the pop-up manufactured by traditional die-cutting processes.

If you are looking for ways to help your printed work stand out, this book is for you.

Be memorable, not ephemeral!

# 01:

## BEFORE YOU START

## 1.1 How to Use the Book

The book explains the basic techniques for creating 3-D pop-ups from one sheet of card that leave large, flat areas of card suitable for adding printed graphics. It is not a book of spectacular white-only pop-ups in the tradition of Origamic Architecture (see 1.2, overleaf), in which each design is full of intricate cut and fold patterns.

Because of this, the projects in the book may look simple or somewhat empty. The book intends to show how the addition of printed graphics will complete a pop-up design, not be an unnecessary or unwanted addition to a design which already looks complete in plain white card. You are encouraged to see past the white card and impose onto it your graphic ideas.

Although many of the techniques are simple by themselves, in combination with other techniques the possibilities can quickly become almost endless and very creative. It is not possible to show all the combinations of all the techniques, so you are strongly encouraged to experiment, to play, to learn from mistakes and to discover for yourself new forms and new technical concepts. Ultimately, this is a book of pop-up possibilities, not a series of templates to copy.

This short opening chapter explains the basics of making pop-ups and should be read carefully. Chapter 2 explains the basic 'Three and One' and 'Two and Two' pop-up configurations. If you are hoping to gain the maximum insight into constructing pop-ups, it is essential to read it and to make many of the examples contained within its pages. The chapters that follow Chapter 2 introduce many new techniques, but also make extensive reference to it. Ignore Chapter 2 at your peril!

As you work through the book, the more examples you make, the better they will be. Pop-ups are dynamic and best understood when played with in the hand, rather than just viewed in a static photograph on the page.

## 1.2 What Is a Pop-up?

Pop-ups are commonly considered to be three-dimensional objects which rise automatically when a sheet of card that has been folded in two is unfolded. Most typically, pop-ups are revealed when the pages of a book are turned and opened to lie flat at 180 degrees. The structures in pop-up books are made from many pieces of shaped card, glued both to each other and to the double-page spread from which they emerge.

There exists another form of pop-up, perhaps lesser known, in which the pop-up is cut and folded from a single sheet of rectangular card that was initially folded in two, then opened to 90 degrees. This form was made popular in the 1980s by a Japanese Professor of Architecture, Masahiro Chatani, who called the technique 'Origamic Architecture' (sometimes called 'Origami Architecture', or simply 'OA'). Professor Chatani created a long series of buildings, abstracts and other pop-ups, mostly using only white card, and his books and exhibitions inspired many designers and amateurs to take up OA. The designs in this book are derived from OA techniques, in that they are made from one sheet of card and each fold opens to 90 degrees (or thereabouts), not to 180 degrees.

While 180-degree book pop-ups create solid-looking forms that can be viewed from all angles, 90-degree pop-ups are often best viewed from one side, or the 'front'. The technique creates 'negative' (or empty) spaces behind sections of card which have been cut and folded to stand forward, so for every negative void there is an equivalent 'positive' of card. This negative/positive interplay of voids and card effectively doubles the visual complexity of a 90-degree pop-up, creating a satisfying richness for even the simplest of designs.

A multi-piece 180-degree pop-up is similar to paper sculpture, but OA is similar to origami: both are metamorphic arts in which a single 2-D sheet of paper or card is transformed into a 3-D form, not additive arts (like 180-degree pop-ups or paper sculpture) in which multiple pieces of card are glued together. This transformation of a single sheet of card into a 3-D form without adding (or losing) any material, is a kind of modern-day 'paper alchemy' that never fails to intrigue or impress.

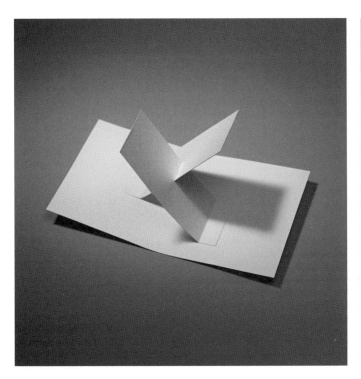

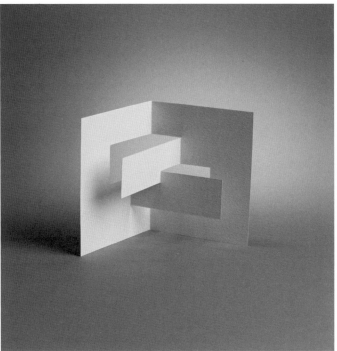

In this example of a 180-degree pop-up, the two arms of the 'X' are made from separate pieces of card and are glued to the unfolded backing sheet. The arms connect together by interlocking short slits on each arm. The result is a form that can be viewed from all angles.

In this 90-degree pop-up, the 'X' motif and the backing card are all made from the same sheet of card. The background cannot fold flat to 180 degrees, as this will also collapse the 'X' flat. The result is a form which needs to be viewed from one side.

### 1.3 How to Cut and Fold

### 1.3.1 Cutting

If you are cutting the card by hand, it is important to use a quality craft knife or, better still, a scalpel. Avoid using the inexpensive 'snap-off' craft knives, as they can be unstable and dangerous. The stronger, chunkier, 'snap-off' knives are more stable and much safer. However, for the same price you can buy a scalpel with a slim metal handle and a packet of replaceable blades. Scalpels are generally more manoeuvrable through the card than craft knives and help you to better create an accurately cut line. Whichever knife you use, it is imperative to change the blade regularly.

A metal ruler or straight edge will ensure a strong, straight cut, though transparent plastic rulers are acceptable and have the added advantage that you can see the drawing beneath the ruler. Use a nifty 15cm ruler to cut short lines. Generally, when cutting, place the ruler on the drawing so that if your blade slips away it will cut harmlessly into the waste card around the outside of the drawing.

It is advisable to invest in a self-healing cutting mat. If you cut on a sheet of thick card or wood, the surface will quickly become scored and rutted, and it becomes impossible to make straight, neat cuts. Buy the biggest mat you can afford. Well looked after, it will last a decade or more.

A scalpel is here shown held in the standard position for cutting. For safety reasons, be sure to always keep your non-cutting hand topside of your cutting hand.

### 1.3.2 Folding

While cutting paper is relatively straightforward, folding is less so. Whatever the method you use, the crucial element is never to cut through the card along the fold line, but to compress the fold line with pressure, using a tool. Whether the tool is purpose-made or improvised is a matter of personal choice and habit.

Bookbinders use a range of specialist creasing tools called 'bone folders'. They compress the card very well, though the fold line is usually 1-2mm or so away from the edge of the ruler, so if your tolerances are small, a bone folder may be considered inaccurate.

A good improvised tool is a dry ball-point pen. The ball makes an excellent crease line, though like the bone folder, it may be a little distance away from the edge of the ruler. I have also seen people use a scissor point, an eating knife, a tool usually used for smoothing down wet clay, a fingernail and a nail file.

A craft knife makes an excellent tool with which to create a fold. Held upside down against the edge of a ruler, it does not cut the card along the length of the fold line, but compresses it.

But my own preference is a dull scalpel blade, or a dull craft knife blade. The trick is to turn the blade upside down. It compresses the card along a reliably consistent line, immediately adjacent to the edge of the ruler.

## 1.4 Equipment

The designs in the book are all simple to measure and to construct. Accuracy in the making is essential, and to achieve this it is important to use equipment that is clean and of reasonable quality.

Here is a list of the basic equipment you will need:
· Hard pencil (2H is good). Keep it sharp
· Good quality eraser (not the one on the end of your pencil)
· Good pencil sharpener if your pencil is not mechanical
· 15cm plastic ruler
· 30cm metal or plastic ruler
· Large 360-degree protractor
· Quality craft knife or scalpel, with replacement blades
· Invisible tape and/or masking tape (for fixing mistakes)
· Self-healing cutting mat, as large as possible

The above equipment – other than the self-healing cutting mat – can be purchased very inexpensively; your total outlay will probably be less than half the price of this book. As with most things, it pays to buy items of quality, though it is more important to use equipment that is inexpensive but clean, rather than equipment that is expensive but dirty. Accumulated grime on a ruler or protractor will quickly transfer to your paper or card and make everything you create look grubby and trivial. Work cleanly and you will work more accurately, with more care and with more motivation.

The one relatively expensive item is a self-healing cutting mat. It is pure vandalism to cut through paper or card on a tabletop and the alternatives of wood or thick card quickly become rutted and problematic. A specialist cutting mat will ensure that every cut line runs straight and smooth. Buy the biggest you can afford. If it is looked after carefully, it will remain in good condition for a decade or more. A nice bonus with a cutting mat is that it will have a grid of centimetres and/or inches printed on, meaning that for some constructions you will rarely, if ever, need to measure with a ruler.

## 1.5 Choosing Card

All the pop-ups in the book have been made using 250gsm card. This isn't a magic weight for pop-ups, but does strike a good balance between strength and flexibility. When you choose your own card, try to work with something between 230 and 270gsm. For pop-ups which are unusually large or unusually small, try heavier or lighter weights.

If you are printing onto your pop-up design, a card with a smooth surface generally prints better than card with a textured surface. If you are printing with a computer printer, your choice of card may be severely restricted. Despite this, if you are using a card recommended for laser or digital printing, the results should not only print excellently but also cut and fold well too.

If you are using a commercial offset printing company to mass-produce your design, then be aware that not all cards that print well will also cut and fold well. Often, less expensive cards can feel somewhat spongy ('aerated') and tend to rip easily. Any pop-up design when manipulated from 2-D to 3-D and back will put a small strain on the point where a cut ends, so if the card is weak, it will tend to rip from that end point. It is better to instead use a more expensive, more compacted card. These cards are usually stronger than aerated card and will cut and fold more reliably. When choosing a card stock, ask for a few small samples and try making pop-ups from them. A preferred card will soon emerge.

If you are die-cutting your pop-up, a three-way discussion between the die cutter, the printer and yourself should help you choose a good all-round card.

If you are making pop-ups by hand, consider using unusual card. The black and white aesthetic of the book may suggest that you should use only white card, but there is no reason why you shouldn't use handmade card, brightly coloured card, textured card, mirrored card, corrugated card, recycled heavyweight paper, junk mail and even thin plastic such as polypropylene, providing – of course – that your choice of material meets the needs of the design brief.

The best way to make an exciting choice of material is to contact a local paper merchant and ask to be sent a set of sample books. If you are a private individual, try to give them the delivery address of a company, so that they are motivated to release their samples for free – they'll think it's a better opportunity for new business than delivering to a private address.

## 1.6 Software

You are strongly urged to make the pop-up samples in the book by hand, at least at first. By working in such a hands-on way, you will come to better understand the structure of how pop-ups work than if they were always drawn using a computer.

Nevertheless, you will sooner or later probably need to draw a pop-up design on a computer, perhaps also adding surface graphics such as text, illustration, or imported images. Pop-up designs, with all their parallel lines, are usually very simple to draw, so any basic vector software will be able to cope very easily with your needs. If you are adding surface graphics, use an appropriate application such as Adobe Illustrator, or one of the many less expensive or freeware alternatives.

**1.7 Symbols**

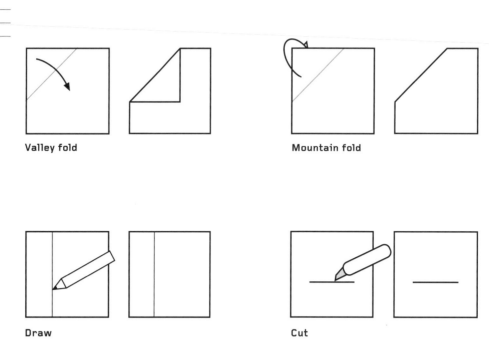

Valley fold

Mountain fold

Draw

Cut

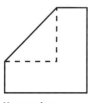

X-ray view

## 1.8 How to Make a Pop-up

### 1.8.1 First, Make a Rough

The temptation when making a pop-up from the book is to make it carefully the very first time. However, you will probably save time in the long run if you first make it roughly, not bothering too much with copying exact measurements or shapes. When this roughly made sample is in your hand, you can quickly understand its structure and then create it more carefully, perhaps making subtle changes so that the cuts and folds work better with your idea.

A further time-saver is to prepare a number of rectangles of card ahead of time so that you can quickly move from one 3-D pop-up 'sketch' to another, as though turning the pages in a sketch pad as you work through a series of ideas. A good general size for practice card is A6 (approx. 15 x 10cm), which is an A4 sheet cut into four rectangles. Save more time by using a supply of ready-cut rectangles, such as postcards or index cards. Blocks of several dozen or even several hundred of these cards can be bought very inexpensively from office suppliers. If you are planning to do a lot of pop-up work, they can save a huge amount of time in cutting larger sheets down to size and so help to make pop-up sketching quicker, more fluent, uninhibited and more fun.

Here's a typical example of a pop-up sketch, which includes areas of pencilled graphics. Note how quickly and freely it has been cut, folded and even repaired with tape.

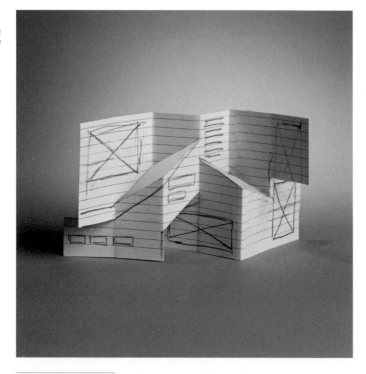

### 1.8.2 Make It Well

When you are happy that a rough 3-D sketch is the one you want to make carefully, then you need to switch your brain from 'sketch mode' to 'precision mode'.

As a general rule, draw the cut-and-fold lines of a pop-up in the same way as you would make a freehand drawing of a figure, still life or landscape, drawing the longest lines first and the shortest lines towards the end. Use your geometric equipment to make sure that lines which should be perpendicular to an edge are exactly so, that measurements which should be equal are exactly so and that parallel lines are parallel. Draw as many construction lines as you wish. You can erase them later.

A strong tip is to erase any unwanted lines before you cut and fold anything, so that only the cut-and-fold lines you need remain visible. This is particularly important for techniques such as 'Piercing the Plane' (see page 92), when only very short fold lines are needed. Check and double-check your folded sketch to be sure that you have erased all the unwanted lines. Use the back edge of your cutting knife to make the folds, as described on page 10. After you have made the fold lines, make the cut lines with your knife, also described on page 10. When all the folds and cuts have been made, carefully erase all the pencil lines.

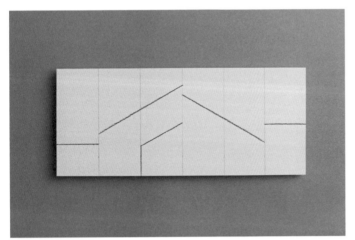

**Step 1**
This is a carefully drawn version of the rough pop-up made overleaf.

Note how all the construction lines are made full length – whether needed or not – creating, in this design, six equal divisions across the card. The heavier lines will be cut.

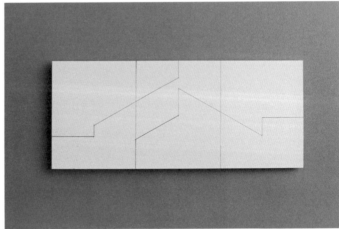

**Step 2**
Erase all the unwanted construction lines, leaving only those lines that will be cut or folded.

Cut and fold the lines according to the instructions on page 10.

### 1.8.3 How to Fold a Pop-up

Transforming a flat sheet of card into a 3-D pop-up can take some exact manipulation. Follow this sequence carefully and it should become an easy process. As with all hand manipulation skills, practice will make perfect.

**1.8.3 _ 1**
To make all the folds, pick up the card and cradle it with both hands. Never try to make the folds with the card flat on the table so that only one side is workable.

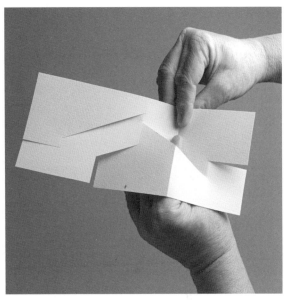

**1.8.3 _ 2**
Be sure to know which folds are mountains and which are valleys. Check with your folded sketch and then double-check. Make the longest folds first.

**1.8.3 _ 3**
Make the shorter folds later, squeezing
the sheet between finger and thumb and
doubling the card back on itself only along
the length of the fold. Do this patiently,
one fold at a time, noting whether it is
mountain or valley.

**1.8.3 _ 4**
If you are sure that all the folds have been
made correctly as mountains or valleys,
then the pop-up can be pressed flat with
all the folds forming simultaneously. To
do this, flatten the folds at the back of
the pop-up first, pressing the paper
slowly flat towards the open ends, as
though folding a sheet of paper in half and
pressing it flat towards the open ends.

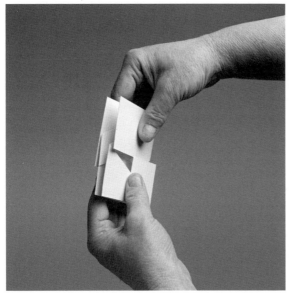

**1.8.3 _ 5**
Continue to flatten the pop-up, taking
care to make creases only where they
are needed.

**1.8.3 _ 6**
This is the collapsed pop-up. Press it flat
to strengthen all the folds. Any errors in
the construction will now be apparent,
as any mismeasurement will not allow the
pop-up to flatten.

**1.8.3 _ 7**
Here is the finished pop-up opened
out to its final position. Compare how
it looks with the initial rough version
seen on page 15. It is quite possible
that something, somewhere, isn't
quite perfect, so be sure to make the
correction next time you draw, fold,
cut and collapse it.

# BASIC
# POP-UP
# FORMS

## 2. BASIC POP-UP FORMS

This chapter is the core of the book and is an essential read for any serious student of one-piece pop-ups. You are strongly advised to work through it slowly, making as many of the examples as you can. If you do, you will begin Chapter 3 with a thorough understanding of what makes a pop-up work, the many possible crease pattern variations for any single cut and how any of the examples can be rotated or flipped for display. Without this understanding of the fundamentals, it may be difficult to design your own pop-ups or to create variations on designs from the book. One tip is, as you make the examples, to write on each what is distinctive about it. By doing so, you will understand more clearly what you have made and be able to compare easily one design against another without reference to the book.

As you will see, it is astonishing how many different pop-up forms can be made from one simple cut. So, although this is a chapter of basic techniques, it is a creative chapter, and a chapter which offers unlimited possibilities. Indeed, if this were the only chapter you were to read, it should give you more ideas than you could ever make, whereas to skip ahead and only read one of the later, showier chapters might severely limit your ability to design a full range of pop-ups.

## 2.1 What Makes a Pop-up 'Pop!'?

Pop-ups are designed and constructed following a few simple principles which must be followed precisely. This spread explains those principles. Although the rules are strict, the book will show how they offer a wealth of creativity.

Only those combinations of folds and cuts described here will create a pop-up that can collapse flat and open to three dimensions, repeatedly. Other combinations may make corrugated surfaces, interesting in their own right, but they will not fold down flat and open to 3-D in the manner of a true pop-up.

**Fold**

**Cut**

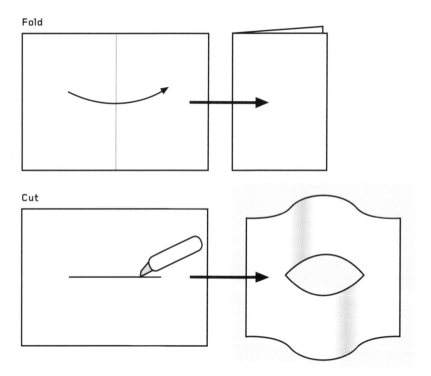

**2.1 _ 1**
A one-piece pop-up is the combination of two contrasting manipulation techniques – folding and cutting. They are contrasting because whereas folding will always contract a sheet, cutting will always open it. They are opposites, yet mutually complementary, like the two sides of a coin.

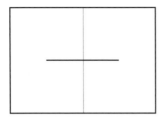

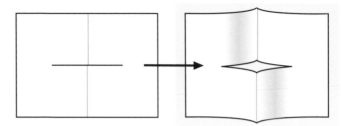

**2.1 _ 2**
To make a pop-up, a fold and a cut must
intersect. They cannot be unconnected.
In its simplest form shown here, the
fold will divide the cut into two equal
halves (this is the 'Symmetrical Pop-up',
described below in this chapter. There is
also an 'Asymmetrical Pop-up', likewise
described below).

**2.1 _ 3**
If the fold above the cut is a valley, it
will be a mountain below the cut, or vice
versa. It cannot be the same fold both
above and below the cut. When both folds
are formed, the card will bend as shown.

**2.1 _ 4**
To complete the pop-up construction,
two additional folds must now be added,
originating from the end-points of
the cut. These folds can either be the
'Three and One' form (three valleys and
one mountain, or three mountains and
one valley), or the 'Two and Two' form
(two valleys and two mountains), both
described in detail, beginning overleaf.

The choice of which crease pattern to use
is at the discretion of the designer. When
flat, the 'Three and One' form hides the
pop-up inside its layers to be revealed
dramatically when the pop-up is opened
to 3-D, whereas when flat, the 'Two and
Two' form already has visible half of the
final 3-D pop-up.

When all the folds have been made
correctly, the card will fold down to
assume its flat position, ready to be
unfolded or 'popped' (hence the term
'pop-up') into 3-D.

**Three and One**

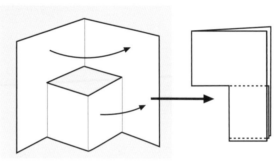

**Two and Two**

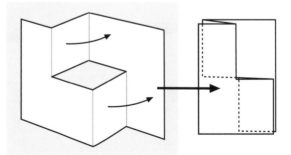

## 2.2 Symmetrical Pop-ups

Symmetrical pop-ups are the most basic form of pop-up construction. The measurements made on one side of the gutter crease are mirrored on the other side, which makes them quick and easy to create, though there is limitless scope for experimentation.

### 2.2.1 Basic Construction

This short section describes in detail how to create the basic pop-up template used later in the chapter and many times later in the book.

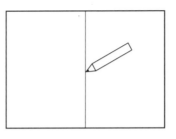

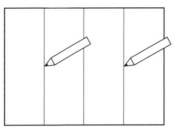

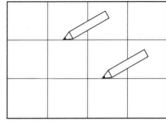

**2.2.1 _ 1**
On a sheet of card, draw a line down the exact centre. This will be the 'gutter crease'.

**2.2.1 _ 2**
Draw two more lines to divide the card into accurate quarters.

**2.2.1 _ 3**
Draw two horizontal lines that divide the card into thirds. They need not be exactly on the thirds.

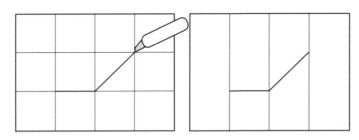

**2.2.1 _ 4**
Draw and then cut a dog-leg angle line as shown. It is essential that the cut begins and ends exactly on the quarter lines.

**2.2.1 _ 5**
Erase the horizontal lines. This is the completed Basic Construction. The precise selection of which vertical lines are used or not used – and which of them become valley folds or mountain folds – will differentiate one pop-up design from another.

### 2.2.2 'Three and One' Variations

There are four possible 'Three and One' variations, depending on which vertical lines are folded. These four variations may be considered the core of all pop-up structures.

**Form One**

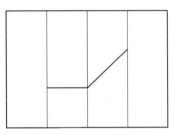

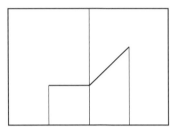

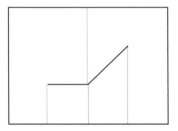

**2.2.2 _ 1**
Begin with the Basic Construction, made in 2.2.1.

**2.2.2 _ 2**
Erase the quarter lines above the dog-leg.

**2.2.2 _ 3**
Create the three valley folds and one mountain fold separately, exactly as shown. Then press all four folds simultaneously to create Form One. The method for making the folds and collapsing the pop-up into shape is described in 1.8.3 (see page 17).

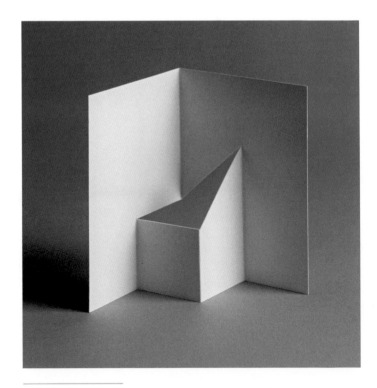

**Form Two**

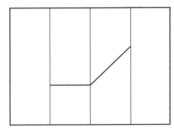 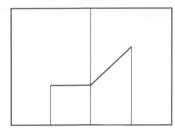 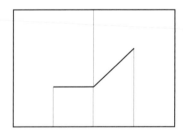

**2.2.2 _ 4**
Begin with the Basic Construction, made
above in 2.2.1.

**2.2.2 _ 5**
Erase the quarter lines above the dog-leg.

**2.2.2 _ 6**
Create the three mountain folds and one
valley fold separately, exactly as shown.
Then press all four folds simultaneously to
create Form Two. The method for making
the folds and collapsing the pop-up into
shape is described above in 1.8.3 (see
page 17).

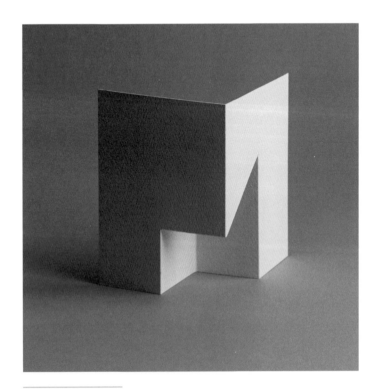

**Form Three**

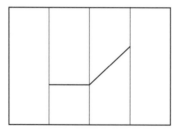 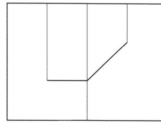 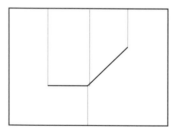

**2.2.2 _ 7**
Begin with the Basic Construction, made above in 2.2.1.

**2.2.2 _ 8**
Erase the quarter lines below the dog-leg.

**2.2.2 _ 9**
Create the three mountain folds and one valley fold separately, exactly as shown. Then press all four folds simultaneously to create Form Three. The method for making the folds and collapsing the pop-up into shape is described above in 1.8.3 (see page 17).

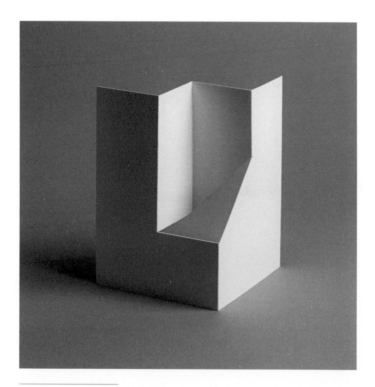

**Form Four**

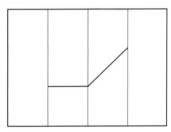

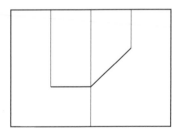

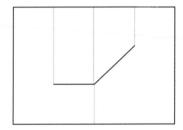

**2.2.2 _ 10**
Begin with the Basic Construction, made above in 2.2.1.

**2.2.2 _ 11**
Erase the quarter lines below the dog-leg.

**2.2.2 _ 12**
Create the three valley folds and one mountain fold separately, exactly as shown. Then press all four folds simultaneously to create Form Four. The method for making the folds and collapsing the pop-up into shape is described above in 1.8.3 (see page 17).

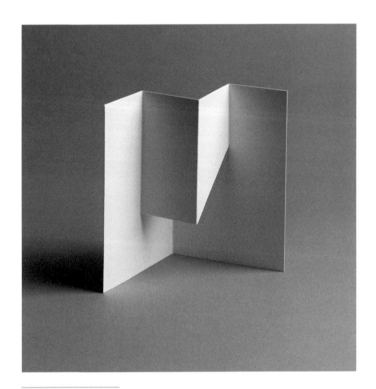

### 2.2.3 'Two and Two' Variations

Again, there are four variations. However, the fold patterns are less intuitive than the 'Three and One' patterns and must perhaps be learnt with a little more diligence.

**Form One**

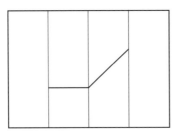

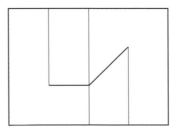

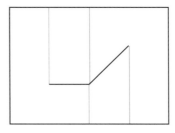

**2.2.3 _ 1**
Begin with the Basic Construction, made above in 2.2.1.

**2.2.3 _ 2**
Erase the right-hand quarter line above the dog-leg and the left-hand quarter line below the dog-leg.

**2.2.3 _ 3**
Create the two valley folds and two mountain folds separately, exactly as shown. Then press all four folds simultaneously to create Form One. The method for making the folds and collapsing the pop-up into shape is described above in 1.8.3 (see page 17).

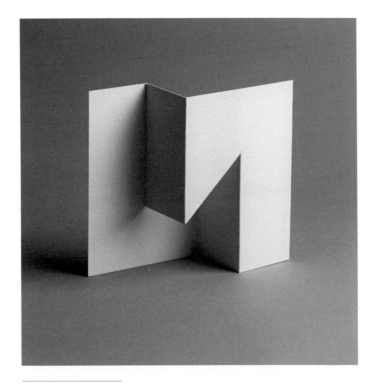

**Form Two**

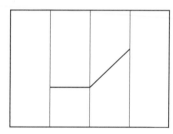 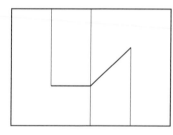 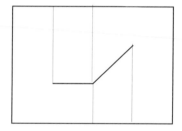

**2.2.3 _ 4**
Begin with the Basic Construction, made above in 2.2.1.

**2.2.3 _ 5**
Erase the right-hand quarter line above the dog-leg and the left-hand quarter line below the dog-leg.

**2.2.3 _ 6**
Create the two valley folds and two mountain folds separately, exactly as shown. Then press all four folds simultaneously to create Form Two. Note that the valley and mountain folds have swapped positions, compared to the pattern above in 2.2.3 _ 3 (Form One). The method for making the folds and collapsing the pop-up into shape is described above in 1.8.3 (see page 17).

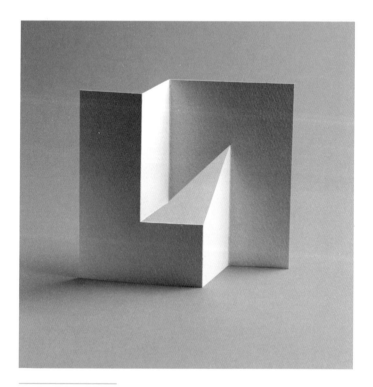

**Form Three**

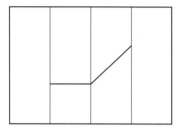 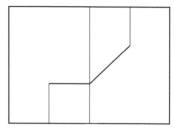 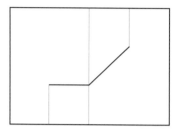

**2.2.3 _ 7**
Begin with the Basic Construction, made
above in 2.2.1.

**2.2.3 _ 8**
Erase the right-hand quarter line below
the dog-leg and the left-hand quarter line
above the dog-leg.

**2.2.3 _ 9**
Create the two valley folds and two
mountain folds separately, exactly
as shown. Then press all four folds
simultaneously to create Form Three.
The method for making the folds and
collapsing the pop-up into shape is
described above in 1.8.3 (see page 17).

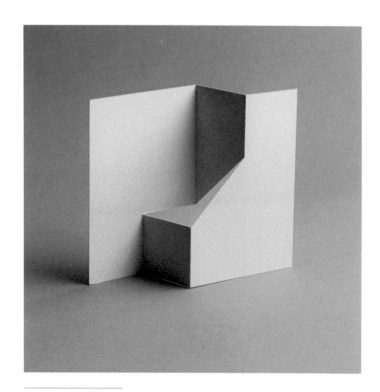

**Form Four**

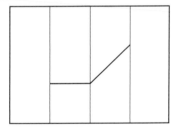

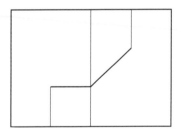

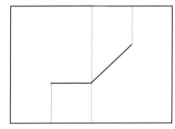

**2.2.3 _ 10**
Begin with the Basic Construction, made above in 2.2.1.

**2.2.3 _ 11**
Erase the right-hand quarter line below the dog-leg and the left-hand quarter line above the dog-leg.

**2.2.3 _ 12**
Create the two valley folds and two mountain folds separately, exactly as shown. Then press all four folds simultaneously to create Form Four. Note that the valley and mountain folds have swapped positions, compared to the pattern above in 2.2.3 _ 9 (Form Three). The method for making the folds and collapsing the pop-up into shape is described above in 1.8.3 (see page 17).

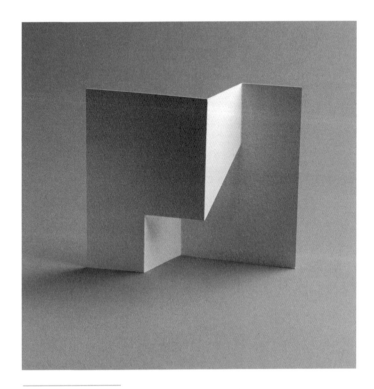

## 2.3 Asymmetrical Pop-ups

Asymmetrical pop-ups require more construction than the simpler symmetrical pop-ups, described above. However, the compensation for the extra work is that they create more visual interest than their symmetrical relatives.

### 2.3.1 Basic Construction

**2.3.1 _ 1**
Before beginning to construct an asymmetrical pop-up, a side-by-side analysis comparing a symmetrical pop-up with an asymmetrical pop-up would be useful.

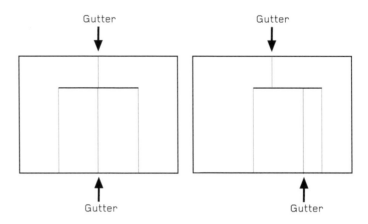

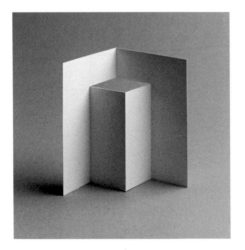

This symmetrical pop-up shows a horizontal cut that extends equally left and right of the gutter, so that the valleys which extend down the card from the ends of the cut are equidistant from the gutter. When popped into 3-D, both pop-up surfaces will be the same size.

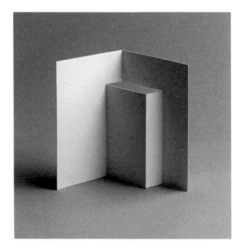

This asymmetrical pop-up shows the cut extending further away from the gutter on the right side than on the left. To compensate for this asymmetry, the mountain fold gutter moves to the right, thus separating the gutter fold into two parts. When popped into 3-D, the two pop-up surfaces will be different sizes (that is, asymmetrical, not symmetrical).

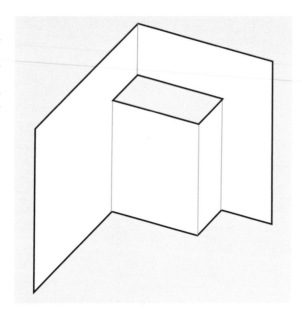

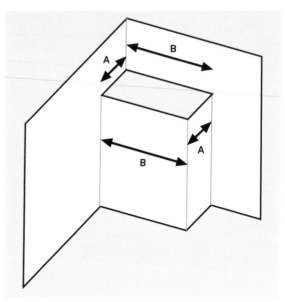

**2.3.1 _ 2**
This is the structure of an asymmetrical
pop-up. Note that the two surfaces of
the pop-up 'box' are of unequal size.

**2.3.1 _ 3**
The two distances marked 'A' must be
equal. The two distances marked 'B' must
also be equal. The construction method
will ensure these distances are equal.

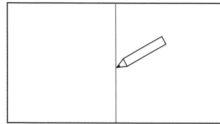

**2.3.1 _ 4**
This is how the distances marked 'A'
and 'B' are arranged on the card. The
following steps explain the construction.

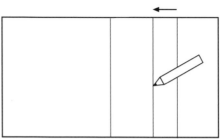

**2.3.1 _ 5**
On a sheet of card, draw a line down the
exact centre. This is the gutter.

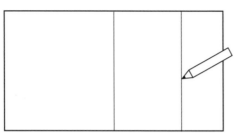

**2.3.1 _ 6**
Draw a line closer to the right-hand edge
than to the centre.

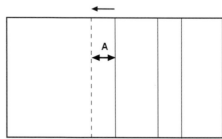

**2.3.1 _ 7**
Draw a line to the left of the second line,
but less than halfway between the line
and the centre line.

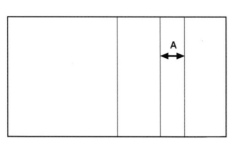

**2.3.1 _ 8**
Measure the distance between the second
and third lines. This is measurement 'A'.

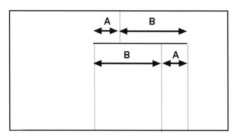

**2.3.1 _ 9**
Measure a distance to the left of the
gutter, which has the measurement 'A'.

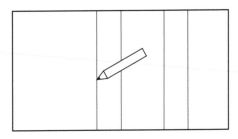

**2.3.1 _ 10**
Draw a line at that distance.

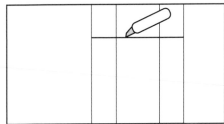

**2.3.1 _ 11**
Cut a horizontal line near the top of the
card which connects the left-hand and
right-hand vertical lines.

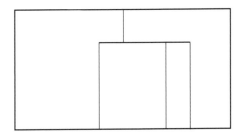

**2.3.1 _ 12**
Erase sections from each of the four
vertical lines, as shown.

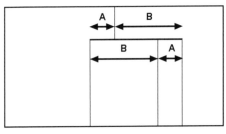

**2.3.1 _ 13**
This is the structure seen in step
2.3.1 _ 4, above. Although the
measurements of 'A' and 'B' may change
relative to each other and the shape of
the cut can be modified, this is the basic
structure of an asymmetrical pop-up.

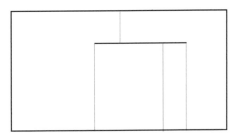

**2.3.1 _ 14**
Create the three valley folds and one
mountain fold separately, exactly
as shown. Then press all four folds
simultaneously to create the final 3-D
form. The method for making the folds
and collapsing the pop-up into shape is
described above in 1.8.3 (see page 17).

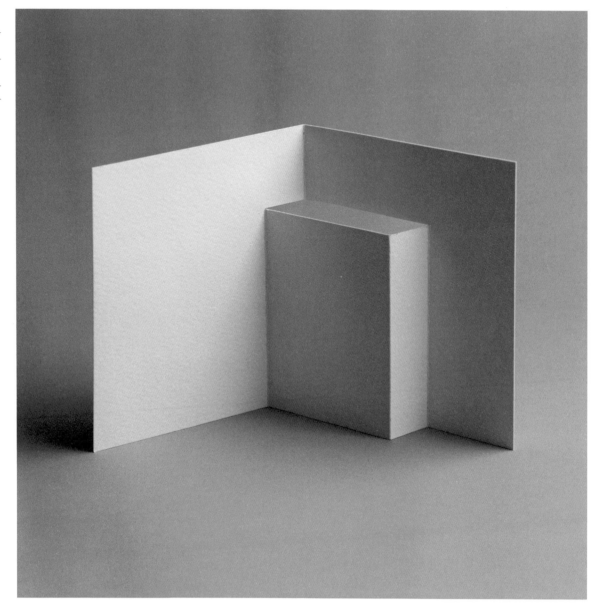

## 2.3.2 Asymmetrical Variations

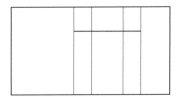

**2.3.2 _ 1**
This is the basic construction for an
Asymmetrical Pop-up, seen above in
step 2.3.1 _ 11. Note how there are four
vertical lines, whereas the construction
for the Symmetrical Pop-up has only
three (see step 2.2.1 _ 5). Despite
this difference in construction, it is
possible to create four different pop-up
structures using exactly the same valley/
mountain crease patterns that were used
for the Symmetrical Pop-ups (see 2.2.2
and 2.2.3, above).

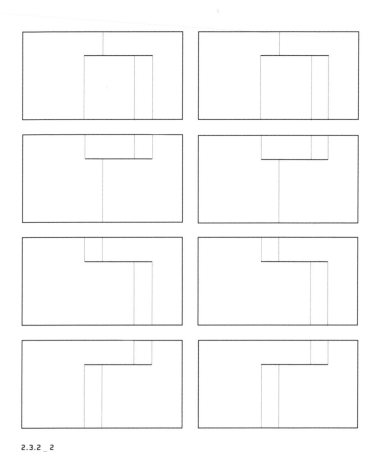

**2.3.2 _ 2**
Here are the four possible pop-up
structures. Note that in each example,
every valley and mountain can be folded
the opposite way, so that the number of
possible variations will double from four
to eight.

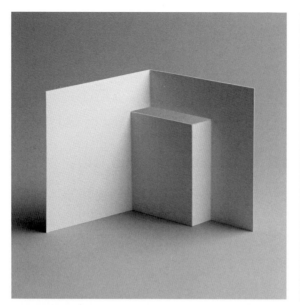

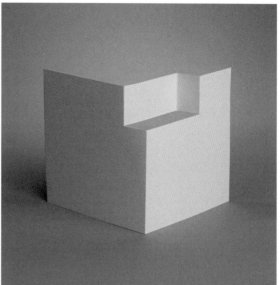

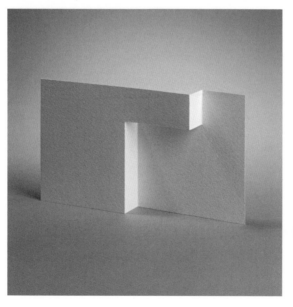

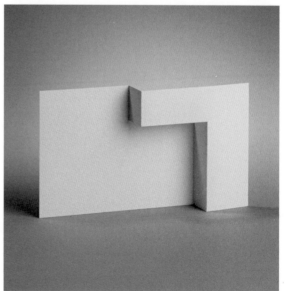

## 2.4 Which Way Up, Which Way Around?

It must be remembered that every pop-up design shown in the book is not unique, but one of a family of at least four, often eight and sometimes twelve. This is because each design can be rotated and reflected – that is, turned upside down, turned over or turned over and turned upside down – so that what may be considered the front side or the top edge is a choice between these four display possibilities.

If the design is asymmetrical, these four possibilities will double to eight. This is because an asymmetrical design can be remade as a mirror image, thus doubling the set of display possibilities for what is essentially the same design. Further, if a pop-up will sit on a flat surface like a letter 'L', then a further two or four display possibilities become available.

So, for each new design that you make, turn it over and around in your hands and view it from all sides. Set it down on a flat surface in a variety of positions, as described above. The design will often change dramatically as it is manipulated from one display position to another and a poor design may suddenly come to life when seen from another frontal point of view.

**2.4**

Here is a simple 'Three and One' example. The pop-up is exactly the same in each drawing – the single cut and the folds are always identical. The top four examples will 'stand' on a flat surface, with the bottom edge always touching the floor. The bottom two examples will 'sit' flat on a surface, like a letter 'L'.

If all the 'Three and One' and 'Two and Two' possibilities for the same dog-leg cut were made and each displayed in one of the four standing positions, the number of different-looking pop-ups for that one cut would be thirty-two. If the cut was mirrored, the total number of different-looking pop-ups when the left-hand and right-hand designs were displayed together would double to sixty-four. That's a remarkably large number of variations. It's amazing that so many design options can be derived from what is – after all – the simplest of pop-up forms. Even the simplest pop-up can offer great potential for creativity, as this example of one cut with sixty-four display possibilities shows.

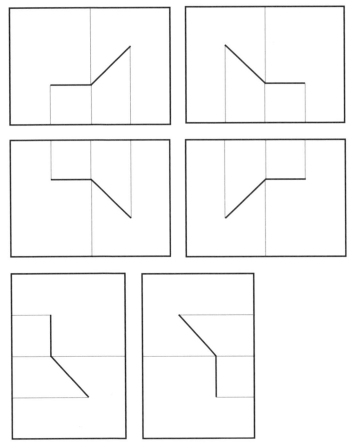

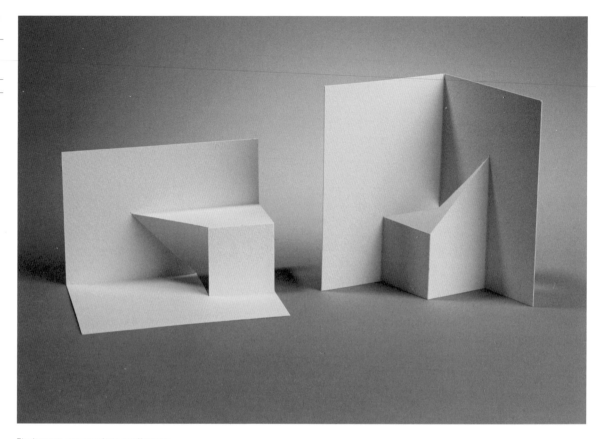

The two pop-ups seen here are the same.
They look different because one is sitting
and the other is standing. Look closely at
illustration 2.4 and you will be able to find
them among the six variations.

# REMEMBER!

To repeat the Introduction:

'this is an inspirational book, not a catalogue'.

Many of the pop-ups which now follow can be made using any of the eight different 'Three and One' and 'Two and Two' crease patterns described above in this chapter, in either the symmetrical or asymmetrical form. Also, each of the eight crease patterns can be rotated and turned so that any pop-up can be stood up and viewed from many different frontal viewpoints.

However, for reasons of space, only one example of the eight (and only one frontal view of it) will henceforth be given.

So, in the chapters that follow, you are strongly encouraged not only to make the single example given, but also to make some of the seven other possible alternative crease patterns and to experiment with frontal viewpoints.

# 03:

## DEVELOPING
## THE BASICS

## 3. DEVELOPING THE BASICS

The previous chapter showed how a single straight cut can create an extraordinary variety of pop-up forms, depending on how the creases are arranged and how a pop-up is displayed. This chapter shows how these simple basics can be developed, while still using just one cut and either the 'Three and One' or 'Two and Two' crease patterns.

It shows how the cut can be changed to become almost any cut line you can imagine, how the shape of the card need not be a simple rectangle, how the size of the pop-up can be changed relative to the size of the card and how the folds need not be parallel to each other. These are not new technical ideas – they will follow in later chapters – but variations on the essential elements that create any pop-up. In combination, these variations will hugely expand your creative possibilities, but without introducing anything fundamentally new.

Please read this chapter with care and make as many of the examples as you can in preparation for Chapter 4.

### 3.1 Taking the Cut for a Walk

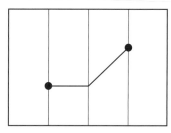

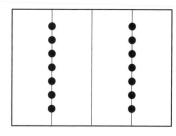

**3.1 _ 1**
The dog-leg cut used throughout the previous chapter begins and ends at the two circled points.

**3.1 _ 2**
However, the dog-leg is only an example. It is possible for the cut to take any continuous path between the same two circled points, or between any point on the left-hand quarter line and the right-hand quarter line, providing an end point is not too close to the top or bottom edge of the card (this will weaken the structure). So, a cut line can connect any circle on the left with any circle on the right.

**3.1 _ 3**
Here are four examples of how the cut can be taken for a walk to connect the two quarter lines. The only limitation is your imagination and the constraints of a brief. It is well worth experimenting with crazy cuts, with cuts that push the limits of what you think may or may not work and to experiment widely with ways of collapsing a pop-up shut with different combinations of valley and mountain folds (see Chapter 2). Note how in the lower two examples, sections of each quarter line have been removed — they are unnecessary.

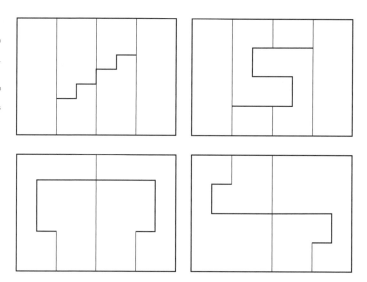

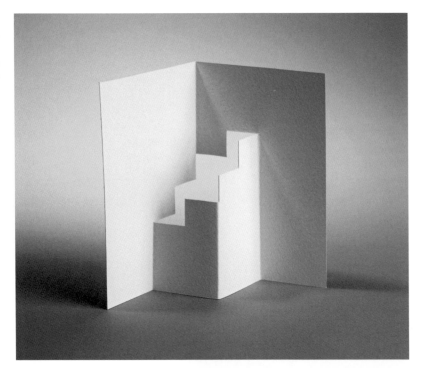

Here are two examples from the four
given opposite.

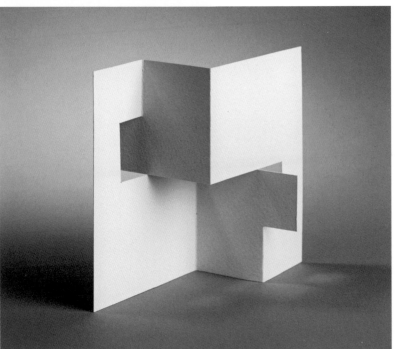

## 3.2 The Shape of the Card

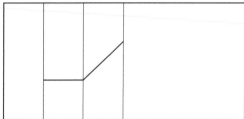

**3.2 _ 1**
The familiar dog-leg cut seen in the left-hand illustration is placed symmetrically on the card. However, the pop-up may be placed anywhere on the card. For example, the right-hand illustration shows the same pop-up construction placed left of centre. Even the simplest pop-up construction will gain interest if placed imaginatively on the card and will create opportunities for an interesting graphic surface.

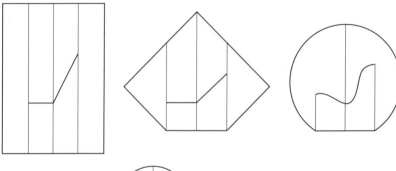

**3.2 _ 2**
These seven examples show progressively how the shape of the card can be made increasingly complex, while retaining even a simple dog-leg cut. The final 'cityscape' example shows how when the cut is taken for a walk (see section 3.1, on page 46) in combination with a creatively imagined silhouette, the possibilities are almost limitless.

Thus, even with just one cut, the endless combinations of the shape of the cut against the shape of the card could provide a lifetime of creative work.

Here are two examples from the seven
illustrated opposite.

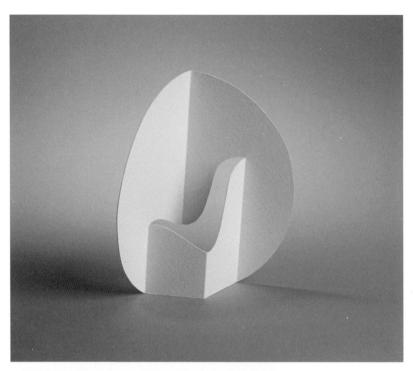

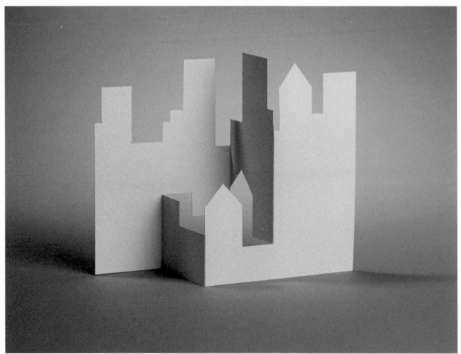

## 3.3 Pop-up Size vs Card Size

Often the most problematic aspect of designing pop-ups is knowing how to measure the size of the pop-up structure against the background card, so that when it is collapsed flat, no small and vulnerable pieces of card will protrude. Sometimes, the background card may need extending to protect these protrusions. This technical section will help with the design of stronger and more secure pop-ups.

**3.3 _ 1**
This is a version of the familiar 'Three and One' structure, seen many times in the book. The pop-up width 'A' is equal to the width of the background card 'B' – the card is divided into quarters. When collapsed flat, the pop-up is contained within the layers of the background card and is held strongly and securely out of sight.

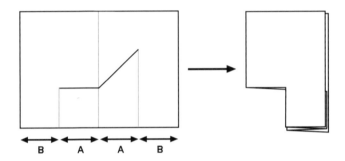

**3.3 _ 2**
Similarly, this version of the 'Two and Two' structure has the card divided into quarters, so that when collapsed flat, the card forms a neat and secure rectangle.

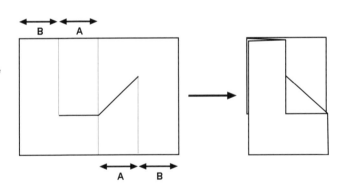

**3.3 _ 3**
In this version of the 'Three and One'
structure, the pop-up width 'A' is less
than the background distance 'B'. When
collapsed flat, the pop-up will be hidden
deep within the layers of the background.
This will give added security to the pop-
up, but it also makes the pop-up structure
smaller and thus less prominent.

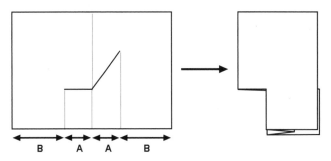

**3.3 _ 4**
Similarly, this version of the 'Two and
Two' structure has 'A' less than 'B'. The
effect when the card is collapsed flat is to
make it wider than when 'A' and 'B' were
equal (see 3.3 _ 2). Thus, opening the
card to reveal the pop-up within will be
less dramatic than 3.3 _ 2.

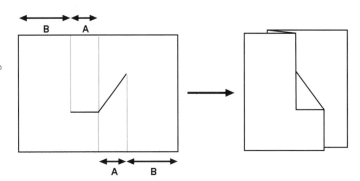

**3.3 _ 5**
In this version of the 'Three-and-One'
structure, the pop-up width 'A' is greater
than the background width 'B'. When
collapsed flat, part of the pop-up will
protrude and be vulnerable.

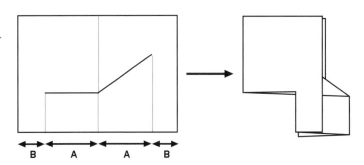

**3.3 _ 6**
Similarly, this version of the 'Two and
Two' structure has 'A' greater than 'B'.
The effect when the card is collapsed
flat is to create a mildly vulnerable form,
which, while not completely secure, may
be considered acceptable.

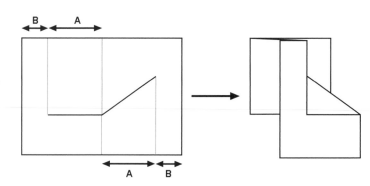

**3.3 _ 7**
Measurements become a little more
complicated when a cut crosses and re-
crosses the gutter, as shown here. This
introduces a new distance 'C'. The crucial
measurement is 'C' against 'B'. Although
the card in this 'Two and Two' structure
is divided into quarters ('A' = 'B'), 'C' is
now greater than 'B'. This means that
when the card is collapsed flat, two small
rectangles will protrude from the card
that are very vulnerable. The solution to
the problem is given in the next step.

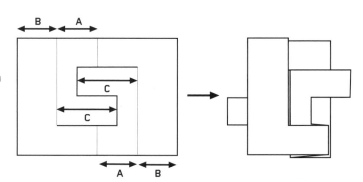

**3.3 _ 8**
Here, 'B' is made wider, so that it has
the same measurement as 'C'. This means
that 'B' has been given a little extra
width, so that when collapsed flat,
the extra backing card covers the
protruding rectangles and makes the
structure strong.

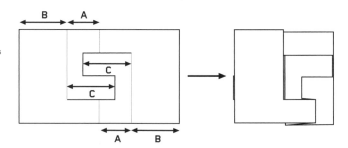

**3.3 _ 9**
A similar problem exists when a 'Three
and One' structure is used. 'C' is again
greater than 'B'. When collapsed flat,
the card assumes a very irregular and
vulnerable shape. The solution to the
problem is given in the next step.

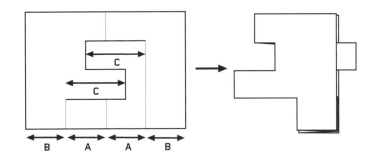

**3.3 _ 10**
The width of 'B' is increased until it is
the same as 'C'. The card is extended on
the right by the distance 'B' + 'C'. This
provides a clean, flat rectangle of card
onto which the layers of vulnerable card
can sit. The new mountain fold could itself
be used as a gutter (see 5.1.1, page 104).

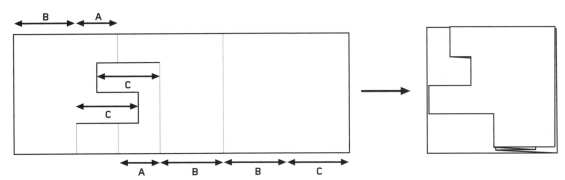

### Conclusion

From these examples, it is clear that any pop-up, when collapsed flat, should
ideally be contained within the background card, or at the very least, have only
a minimally vulnerable silhouette. Any problem is solved simply by extending the
width (and in some cases the height) of the backing card.

### 3.4 Non-parallel Folds

The traditional structure for a one-piece pop-up is to have all the folds
vertical and parallel both to each other and to the edges of the card. However,
with a little creative measurement, the folds can remain parallel but not be
vertical on the card, or can converge in symmetrical or asymmetrical ways.
These techniques can create structures of great originality, very different to
the boxy look of more conventional pop-ups.

### 3.4.1 Not Parallel to the Edge

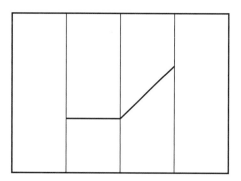 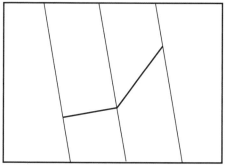

**3.4.1 _ 1**
The familiar dog-leg cut-and-fold pattern
is shown in the left-hand illustration. The
right-hand illustration shows the same
pattern, but rotated off the vertical.
Note that all the folds remain parallel to
each other, but are not now square to the
edges of the card. The construction can
be cut and folded to look like any of the
eight 'Three and One' or 'Two and Two'
structures shown in Chapter 2.

3.   DEVELOPING
     THE BASICS
**3.4  Non-parallel
     Folds**
3.4.1 Not Parallel
     to the Edge

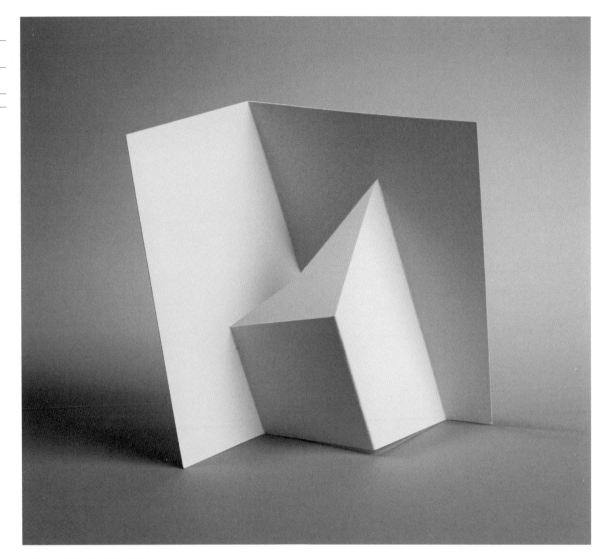

In this example, the sloping pop-up
stands with great stability. However,
depending on the angle of the slope and
thus the degree to which the pop-up
is tipping over, not all non-parallel
pop-ups will stand. Thus, some degree
of experimentation may be necessary to
achieve a stable form.

### 3.4.2 Converging Folds: Symmetrical

Converging folds create pop-up forms of great asymmetry and dynamism. They must be constructed with care, particularly with regard to the size of the pop-up against the backing sheet, as described in 3.3 on page 50. Once mastered, this technique will quickly become a favourite.

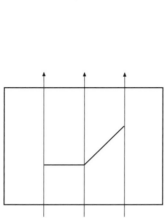

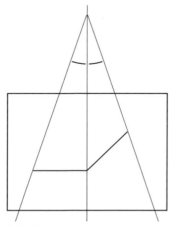

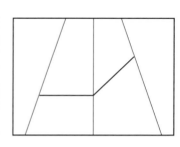

**3.4.2 _ 1**
This is the familiar dog-leg cut-and-fold pattern. Note that all the folds are parallel.

**3.4.2 _ 2**
This is the same pattern, but now the left and right folds converge on the vertical centre line (the gutter). The point of convergence may be higher or lower than shown, but must be on the centre line. To draw this construction, it may be helpful to fix the card to a backing sheet of paper and to draw on the backing sheet. The equal angles can be measured with a protractor, or more simply by marking two points along the bottom edge of the card, equidistant from the centre line, then connecting them to the point of convergence.

**3.4.2 _ 3**
This is the completed Basic Construction.

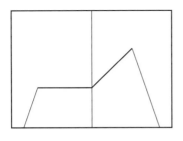

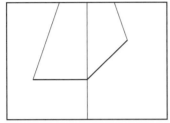

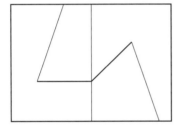

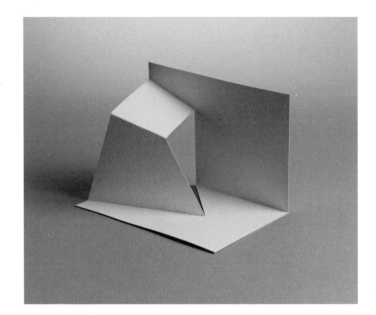

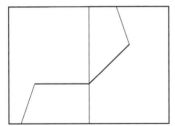

**3.4.2 _ 4**
These are the four basic 'Three-and-
One' and 'Two-and-Two' crease patterns
which can be created from the basic
construction. Refer to Chapter 2 for
full details.

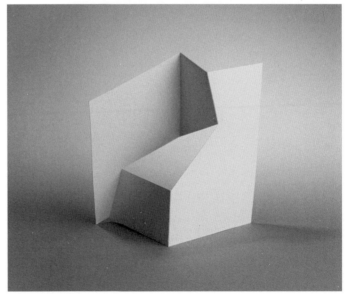

Here are two examples from the 4 given
in illustration 3.4.2 _ 4. Note that one
is sitting. The disruption to the edge on
the left created by the converging folds
means that it will not stand upright.

### 3.4.3 Converging Folds: Asymmetrical

This is the most complex of one-cut constructions, but creates highly sophisticated-looking structures. Follow the method with care. It is essentially the same as the 'Asymmetrical Pop-ups' construction, on page 37.

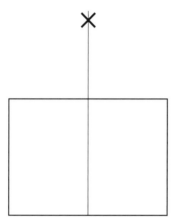

**3.4.3 _ 1**
Draw a centre line on a sheet of card.
Continue that line upwards, perhaps on a
sheet of paper placed under the card. Fix
the card and the paper together, so that
they cannot move. Mark an 'X', which is
the point of convergence for all the folds.

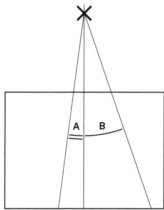

**3.4.3 _ 2**
Measure two different angles, 'A' and 'B'.
Draw the lines.

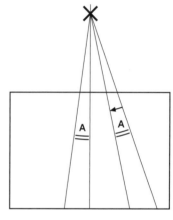

**3.4.3 _ 3**
Draw a fourth line. Its placement is closer
to the centre line than the right-hand
line drawn in 3.4.3 _ 2 and – crucially –
it creates a copy of angle 'A'.

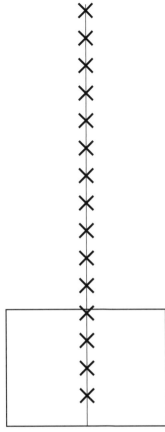

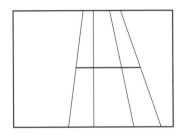

**3.4.3 _ 4**
This is the completed construction. The
simple horizontal cut may be a different
shape (see 'Taking the Cut for a Walk',
page 46), but the organization of the
angles is fixed. Note that angle 'A' is
seen twice, on the left and on the right.

**3.4.3 _ 5**
The point of convergence can be
anywhere on the centre line (the gutter).
It is well worth experimenting with
different placements of this point, for
both the symmetrical and asymmetrical
convergent structures.

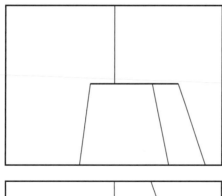

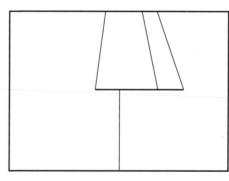

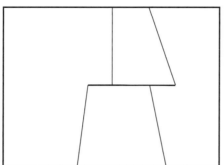

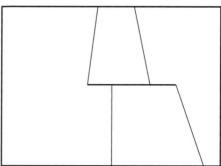

**3.4.3 _ 6**
Here are the four basic 'Three and One'
and 'Two and Two' crease patterns
which can be created from the Basic
Construction. Refer to Chapter 2 for
full details. Note that when made and
collapsed flat, the angled folds will not
create a neat, rectangular, flat silhouette
of card. Some adaptation of the shape of
the card may be necessary to keep the
collapsed pop-up from being vulnerable
(see '3.3 Pop-up Size vs Card Size', on
page 50).

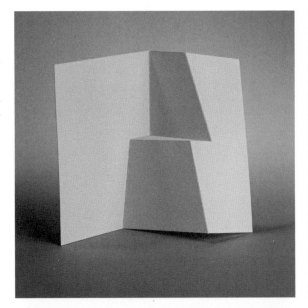

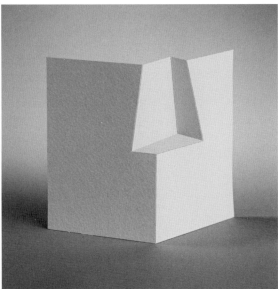

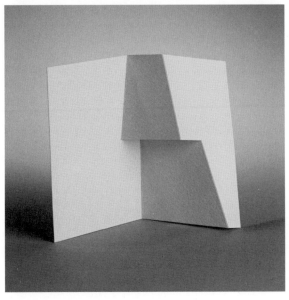

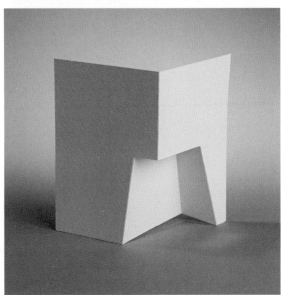

The four examples shown here are
derived from the illustrations opposite.
However, they are not the full set of
possibilities. Each example could have its
valley folds swapped for mountains and its
mountains swapped for valleys, to create
a further four variations. The diligent
student may discover other 'Two and Two'
variations, not shown here.

# 04:
## RELEASING THE FOLDED EDGE

4.  RELEASING
    THE FOLDED
    EDGE

This chapter introduces a series of new pop-up techniques, each designed to open out a basic pop-up form by cutting into and away from a crease. The experienced student of pop-ups will recognize that many of these techniques are not commonly used in conventional Origamic Architecture (OA) structures, where cuts along a crease or to the edge of the card are rarely made, if ever. The effect of these unconventional techniques is to dissolve the 'greetings card' aesthetic of OA to create structures which have many large, flat facets suitable for using as the ground for surface graphics.

In many ways then, this chapter is the most original in the book. Worked through carefully, it will enable you to place graphics on a large number of disconnected surfaces to create an effect that is both dynamic and very three-dimensional. Further, whereas what was learnt in the previous chapters was a series of precisely engineered structures that would fold flat only if exact instructions were followed, the cutting techniques introduced in this chapter are much more intuitive.

Please read this chapter with care and make as many of the examples as you can before moving on to Chapter 5.

### 4.1 The 'Fold to Fold' Cut

This versatile and simple cutting technique releases the card along a section of any crease, to create a pleasingly complex cut-edge shape where previously there had been a simple fold.

The cut shapes shown here are all rectangular, but the shape can be anything you can imagine.

### 4.1.1 The Basic Technique

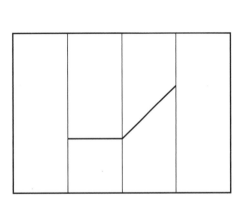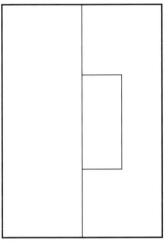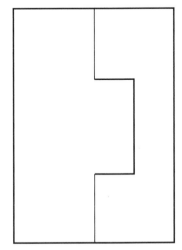

**4.1.1 _ 1**
This is the familiar dog-leg cut-and-fold pattern, used before. Note there are three creases. Each crease is divided into upper and lower sections, separated by the cut. Thus, there are six sections of crease. The 'Fold to Fold' cut described here can be placed on any of these sections and on any number of the sections.

**4.1.1 _ 2**
To make a basic example, draw a line down the centre of a sheet of card. Then, draw a rectangular line which begins and ends exactly on the line.

**4.1.1 _ 3**
Erase the centre line between the two ends of the rectangular line. Cut the rectangle, ensuring that the cut begins and ends exactly on the centre line.

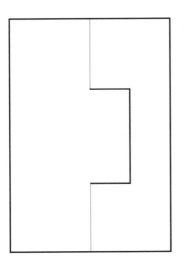

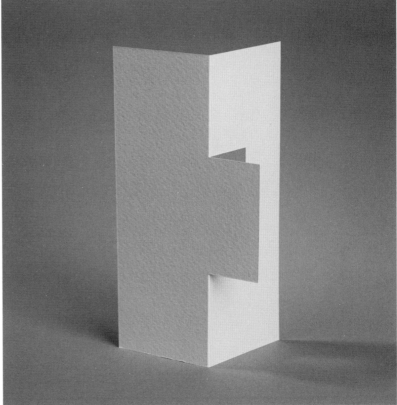

**4.1.1 _ 4**
Crease the upper and lower sections of
the centre line as a mountain. When the
crease is folded, the rectangle will stand
away from the card on the right. Never
crease between the ends of the cut, as
this will spoil the visual effect.

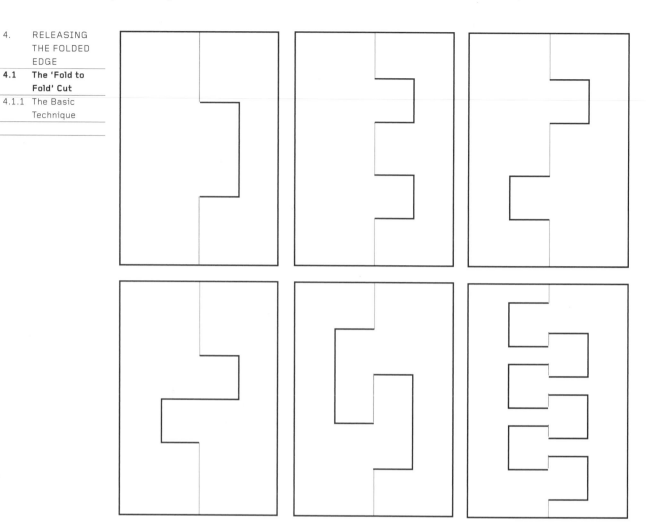

**4.1.1 _ 5**
Here are six variations of increasing
complexity. The rectangular cut can be
made once or more than once. Multiple
rectangles can be separate, joined to
make an 'S'-type cut, or overlap each
other. When overlapped, note how
the small creases which connect the
rectangular cuts are valleys,
not mountains.

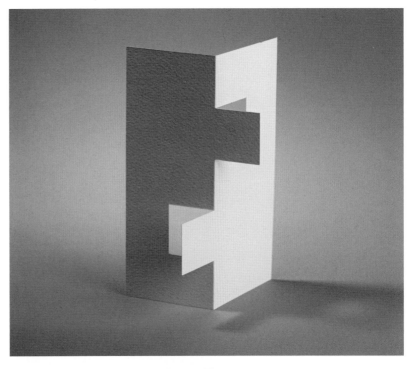

These are two examples from
the six shown opposite.

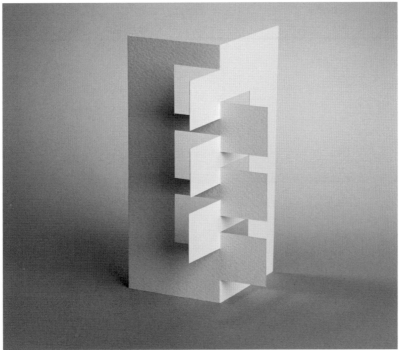

### 4.1.2 Applying the Technique

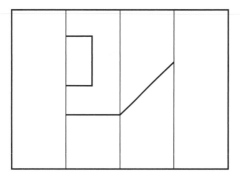

**4.1.2 _ 1**
Here, the rectangle is placed on the
upper left-hand crease of the familiar
dog-leg construction. Note how it sits
comfortably, away from the dog-leg cut
and from the top edge of the card.

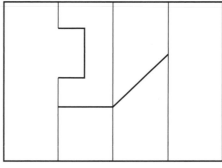

**4.1.2 _ 2**
Erase the line inside the rectangle. This is
the final construction, ready to be cut and
folded to make a pop-up.

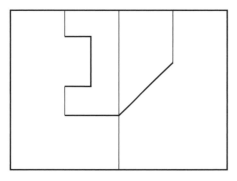
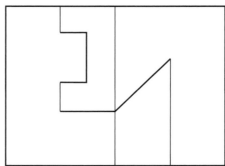

**4.1.2 _ 3**
Here are the two possible arrangements
of the creases. The left-hand illustration
shows the 'Three and One' pattern and
the right-hand illustration shows the 'Two
and Two' pattern. Each pattern can be
folded in two possible ways, depending
on which creases are made as valleys
and which are made as mountains. See
sections 2.2.2 and 2.2.3 in Chapter 2,
for full details (if you have not made
the examples in these sections, you are
recommended to do so).

4. RELEASING
   THE FOLDED
   EDGE

**4.1  The 'Fold to
     Fold' Cut**

4.1.2  Applying the
       Technique

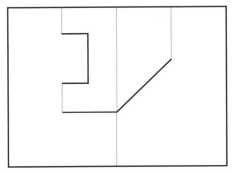

**4.1.2 _ 4**
Here are the four possible
crease patterns.

The two photographs
show the first and fourth
examples.

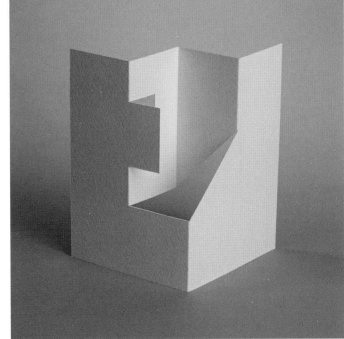

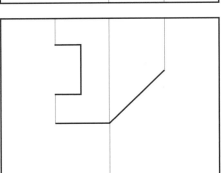

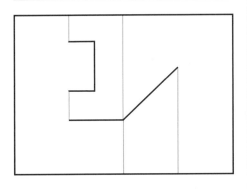

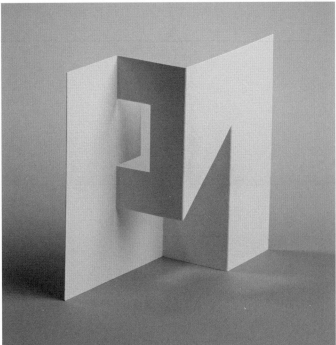

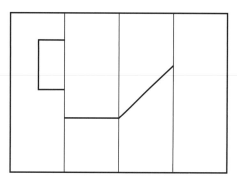

**4.1.2 _ 5**
Here, the rectangle is placed on the other
side of the top left-hand crease.

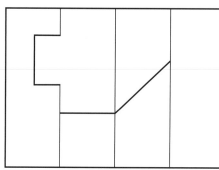

**4.1.2 _ 6**
Erase the line inside the rectangle.

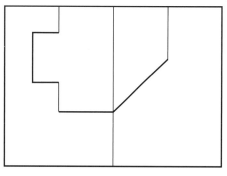

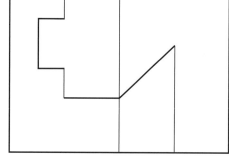

**4.1.2 _ 7**
Similarly, there are two possible
arrangements of the creases. Note
that they are the same as in 4.1.2 _ 3
on page 68 and the same comments apply.

4.      RELEASING
        THE FOLDED
        EDGE

**4.1   The 'Fold to
        Fold' Cut**

4.1.2  Applying the
       Technique

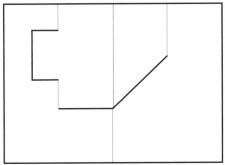

**4.1.2 _ 8**
Here are the four possible
crease patterns.

The photos show the first
and fourth examples.

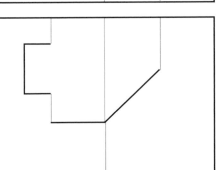

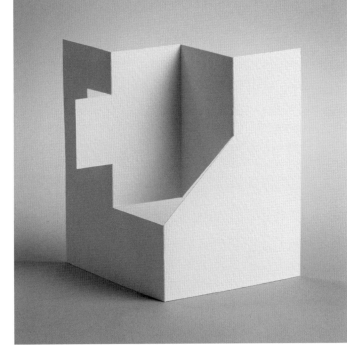

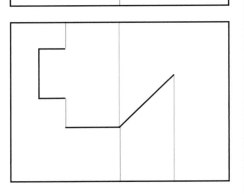

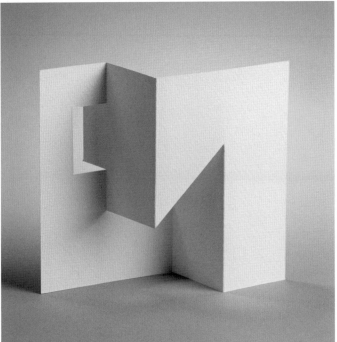

### 4.1.3 Multiple Cuts

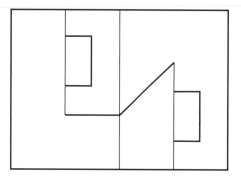

**4.1.3 _ 1**
The rectangular cut can be repeated
elsewhere on the card. Here is one
example of how two rectangles may be
arranged, though there are many others.

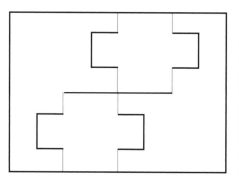
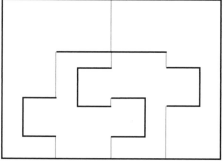

**4.1.3 _ 2**
A maximum of four rectangles may be
used on any 'Three and One' or 'Two
and Two' pattern, one on each crease.
There are many possibilities for complex
arrangements, especially if overlapping
multiples are arranged on one crease
(see 4.1.1 _ 5, page 66).

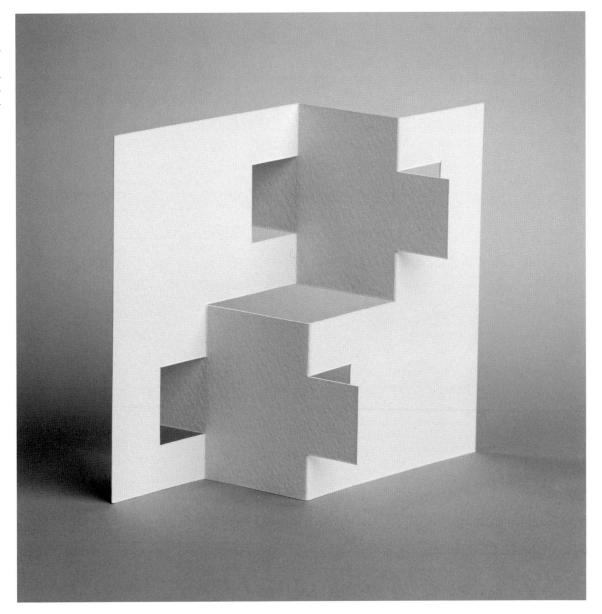

This is the left-hand illustration in
4.1.3 _ 2, opposite.

4.    RELEASING
      THE FOLDED
      EDGE

4.1   The 'Fold to
      Fold' Cut

4.1.4  The Pop-up Size

### 4.1.4 The Pop-up Size

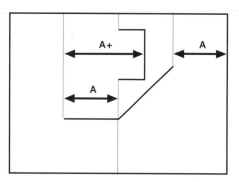

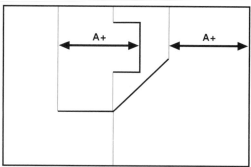

**4.1.4 _1**
The addition of a rectangular cut on
a section of the gutter crease will
increase the width of 'A' to 'A+'. Thus,
when the card is collapsed flat, the cut
rectangle will protrude from the side and
be vulnerable (see section 3.3, Pop-up
Size vs Card Size, page 50, for a full
explanation).

**4.1.4 _2**
If the rectangular cut is on a mountain
gutter fold, increase the width of the
background card from 'A' to 'A+'.
This extra width will protect the
protruding rectangle.

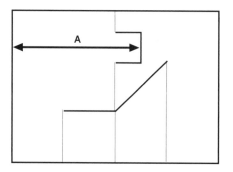

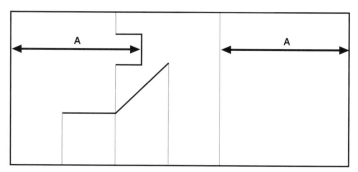

**4.1.4 _3**
If the rectangular cut is made on a valley
gutter, it is necessary to add a large
section of card on the right (or on the
left) to protect it, equal to distance 'A'.
This may be considered an extravagance,
but it also creates an extra clean,
graphic surface.

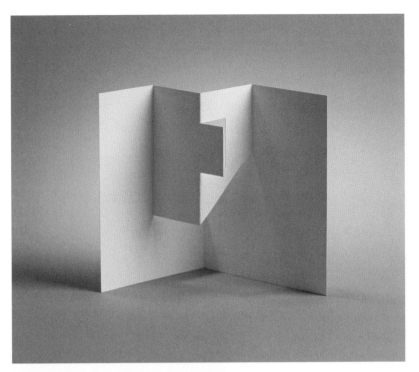

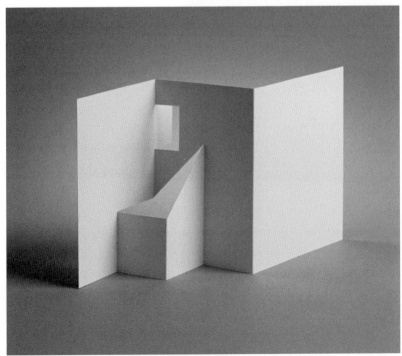

## 4.2 The 'Fold to Edge' Cut

Instead of making a cut that begins and ends on a crease, it is also possible to make a cut that begins on a crease but ends at the edge of the card. The effect is to open the card into a series of dynamic intersecting planes, creating an effect far removed from the traditional pop-up blocks seen in Chapter 2.

### 4.2.1 Cuts to the Side Edge

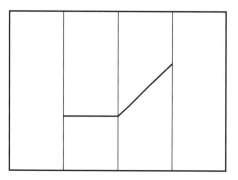

**4.2.1 _ 1**
Here is the familiar dog-leg construction. Note again that the three creases are each divided into two sections. The 'Fold to Edge' cut can be placed on any of these six creases.

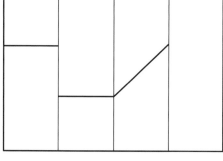

**4.2.1 _ 2**
In this example, the cut begins on the upper left-hand crease and extends to the left-hand edge of the card.

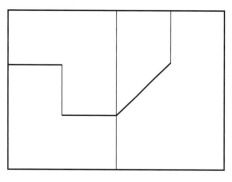
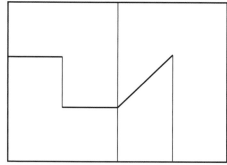

**4.2.1 _ 3**
When the unwanted construction lines are removed, the familiar 'Three and One' and 'Two and Two' constructions can be made, each in two forms, depending on the arrangement of the valleys and mountains (see 2.2, page 24).

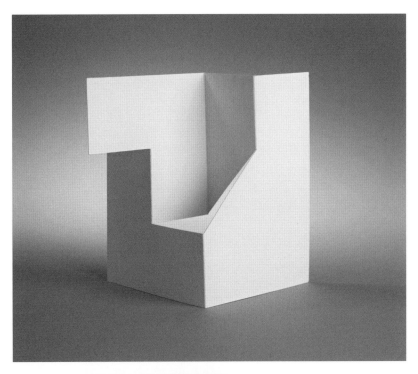

These two examples are shown opposite
in 4.2.1 _ 3. Two further examples could
be made if all the mountain and valley
folds were reversed.

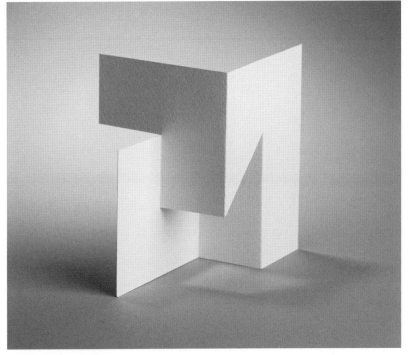

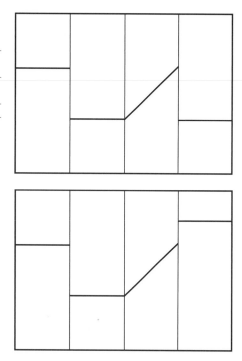

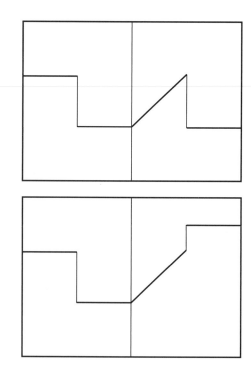

**4.2.1 _ 4**
It is also possible to add a 'Fold to
Edge' cut at the right of the pop-up. The
drawing at the top shows the cut below
the dog-leg; the drawing beneath shows
the cut above the dog-leg.

**4.2.1 _ 5**
When the unwanted construction lines are
removed, the familiar 'Three and One' and
'Two and Two' constructions can be made,
each in two forms, depending on the
arrangement of the valleys and mountains
(see 2.2, page 24).

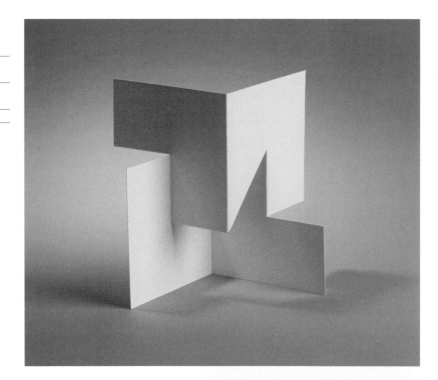

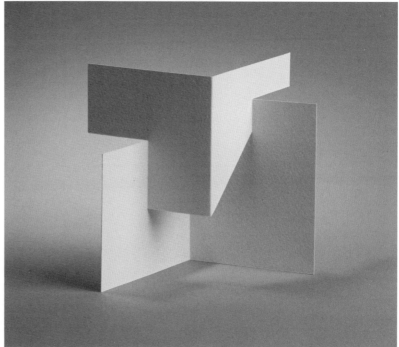

## 4.2.2 Cuts to the Top and Bottom Edges

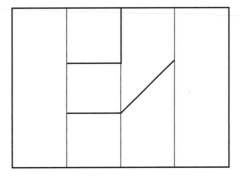

**4.2.2 _ 1**
The cut can also travel from any fold to
the top or bottom edge. In this example,
the cut travels from the upper left-hand
fold to the gutter, then upwards to the
top edge.

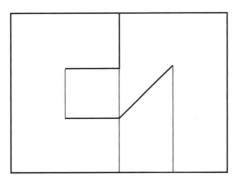

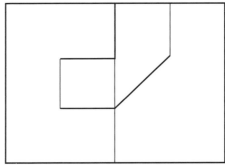

**4.2.2 _ 2**
When the unwanted construction lines are
removed, the familiar 'Three and One' and
'Two and Two' constructions can be made,
each in two forms, depending on the
arrangement of the valleys and mountains
(see 2.2, page 24).

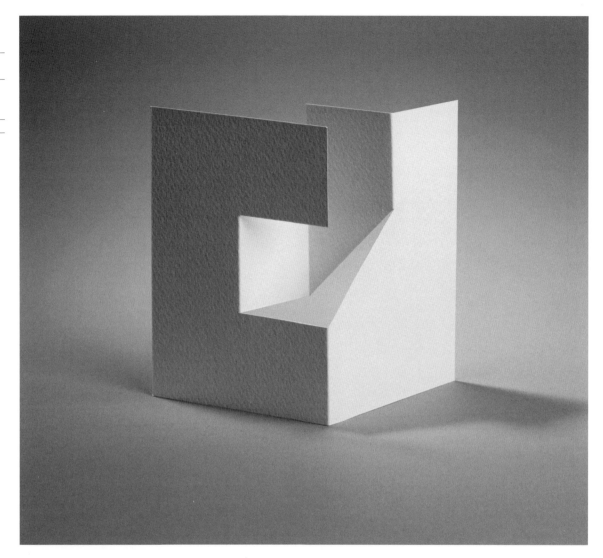

This is the lower right illustration, shown
opposite. It could also be made with all
the mountain and valley folds reversed.

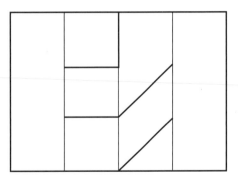 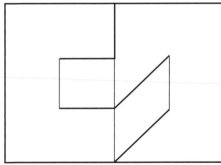

**4.2.2 _ 3**
A second cut can be introduced, either to
the same edge, or to the opposite edge (the
bottom edge), as here. The construction
can only be a 'Two and Two' crease
pattern, though it can have two forms,
depending on the arrangement of the
valleys and mountains (see 2.2, page 24).

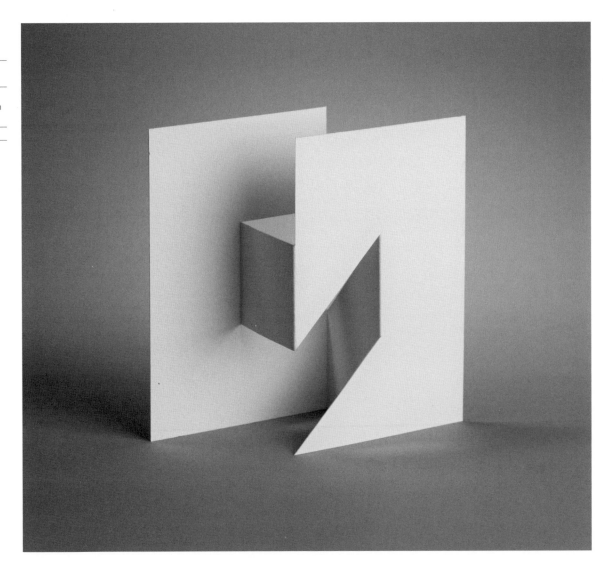

### 4.2.3 Cuts to Any Edge

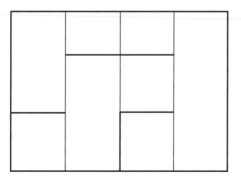

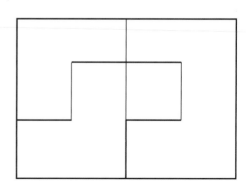

**4.2.3 _ 1**
The technique works particularly well
when cuts are taken to a combination
of side and top/bottom edges. In this
example, cuts are taken from the quarter
lines to the left-hand and bottom edges.

**4.2.3 _ 2**
When the unwanted construction lines
are removed, the familiar 'Three and One'
construction can be made in two forms,
depending on the arrangement of the
valleys and mountains (see 2.2, page 24).

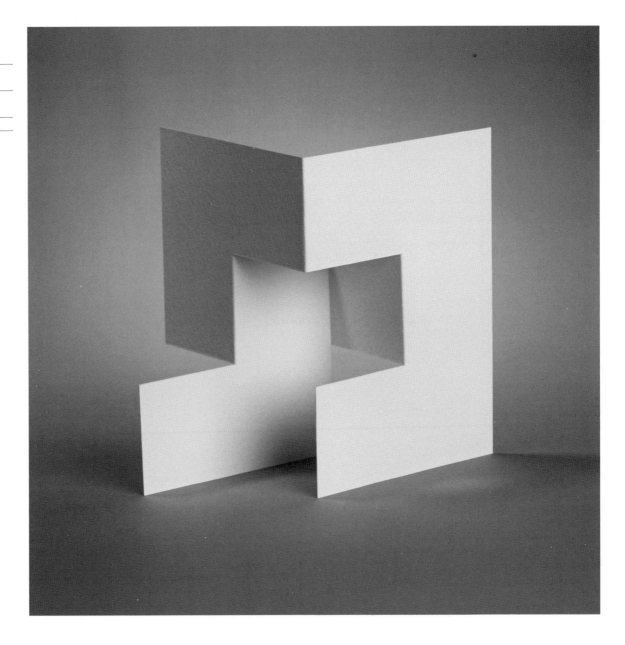

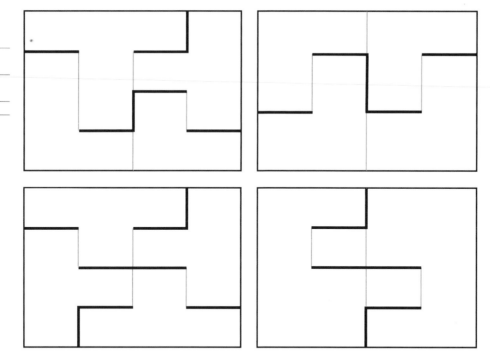

**4.2.3 _ 3**
Many other combinations of cuts can be
made, to any number of edges. When the
shapes of the cuts are changed to any
creative silhouettes you can imagine, then
the technique is not only versatile, but
also very creative.

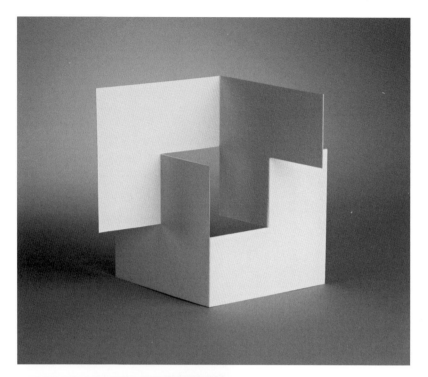

These two pop-ups are illustrated opposite, at the top right and bottom right.

## 4.3 Piercing the Plane

This technique involves more cutting and folding than seen before in the chapter, but it creates a pleasing ambiguity between what may be regarded as the 'front' and the 'back'. This technique is particularly useful for making a pop-up that needs to be viewed from all angles, not just from the front.

### 4.3.1 Half Construction

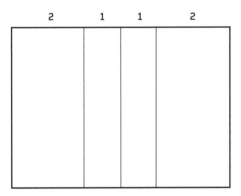

**4.3.1 _ 1**
These are the basic measurements. Instead of dividing the paper into quarters as before, the lines to the left and right of the gutter are now placed one-third of the way between the gutter and the side edges of the card.

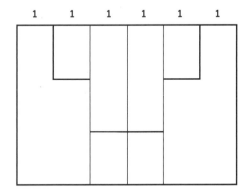

**4.3.1 _ 2**
This is not a full construction, but only half, involving the making of just one cut across the gutter, instead of the two. Two additional cuts are made from the side lines to the top edge. Note how the card is divided into equal sixths across its width. This division will remain for the other constructions in this section.

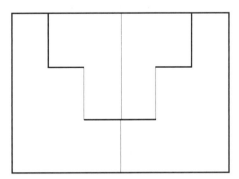

**4.3.1 _ 3**
This is the final half construction. It bears some relation to the constructions in the previous section. Notice how the 'V' across the top edge is orientated in the opposite direction to the remainder of the card.

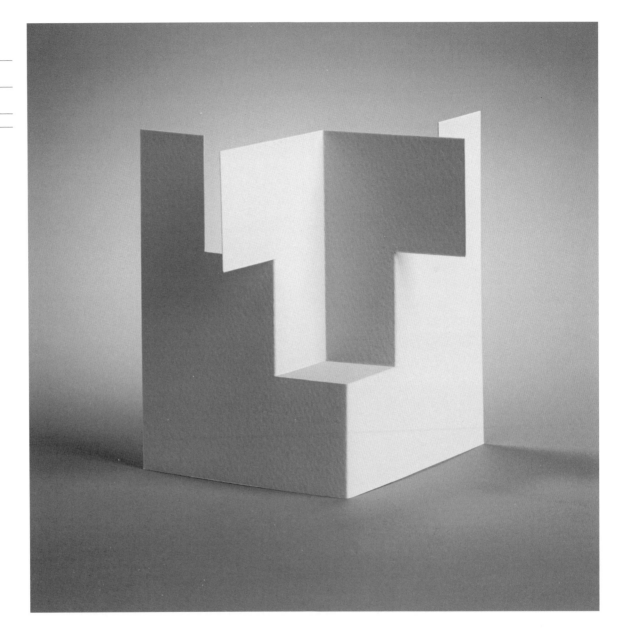

## 4.3.2 Full Construction

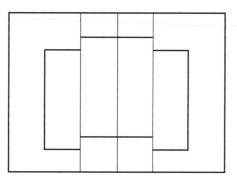

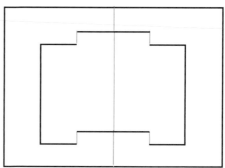

**4.3.2 _ 1**
The full construction seen here is in two parts. The first part consists of two cuts across the gutter (the Half Construction, above, had just one cut). The second part is the two rectangular 'wings' on the left and right of the card. In this example, the wings are dropped below the two cuts that cross the gutter.

**4.3.2 _ 2**
This is the final construction. Note that the entire vertical gutter line remains, but the long construction lines left and right of the gutter have been reduced to just two short sections each. The remarkable effect of this is to create a large 'V' of card which pierces the background, a perfect surface for the application of surface graphics.

Here is the result. The pop-up looks equally good when viewed from the back, when the 'V' becomes more prominent.

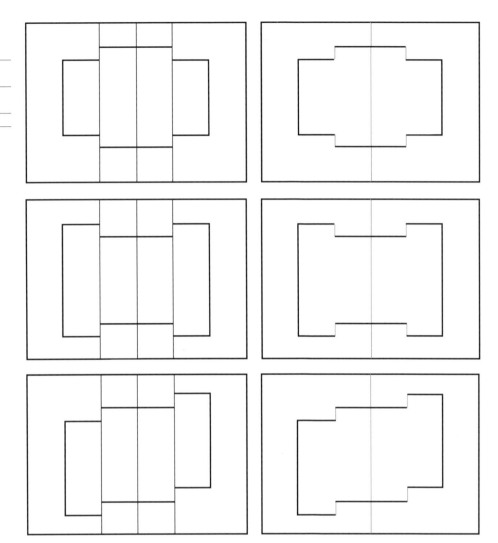

**4.3.2 _ 3**

Here are the three other ways in which
the wings can relate to the two cuts
across the gutter.

Top: both wings are within the two lines
across the gutter.

Middle: both wings are outside the two
lines across the gutter.

Bottom: the left-hand wing is below the
two lines across the gutter and the
right-hand wing is above.

Notice that the four short folds in each
construction are valleys and mountains
in different combinations.

**4.3.2 _ 4**
Here are a series of variations. The
constructions are on the left and the
completed cut and fold patterns are on
the right. The silhouette of the shape in
the middle can be simple and geometric,
as shown in these examples, or it can be
as complex as can be imagined. It could
even be a representational silhouette,
such as a letterform, a bird, a building
or a train.

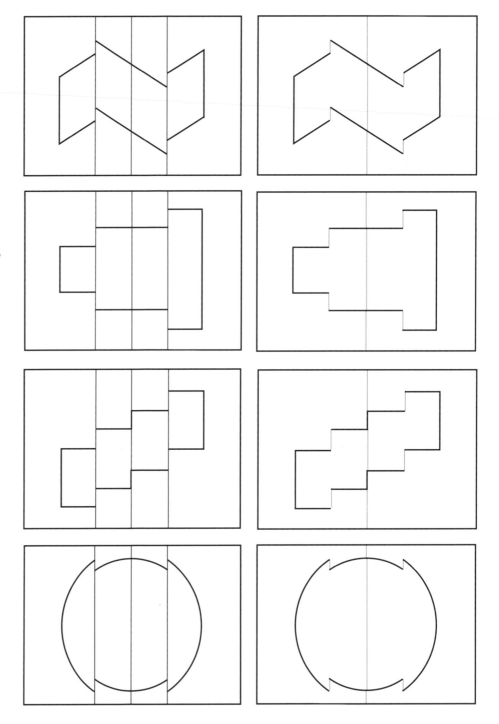

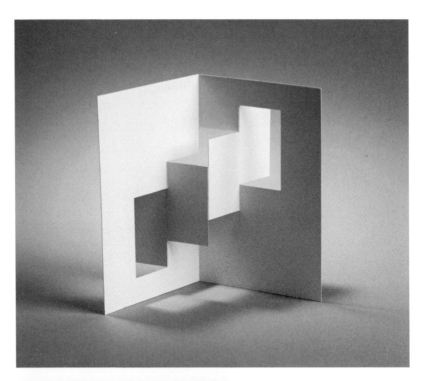

These two pop-ups are the lower two, illustrated opposite.

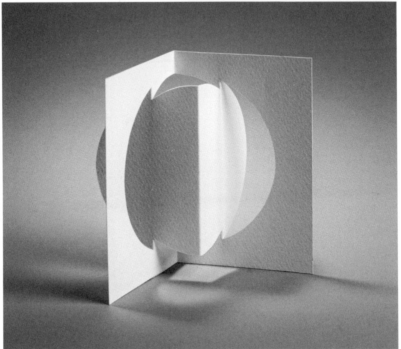

### 4.3.3 No Wings

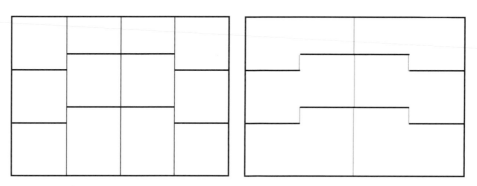

**4.3.3 _ 1**
The wing cuts at the left and right can be
eliminated, replaced by two cuts on each
wing, which extend to the edge of the
card. These cuts can be placed in any of
the four positions seen in 4.3.2 _ 2 and
4.3.2 _ 3.

This is one of the most unusual designs in the book, featuring only a few very short folds, but unusually long cuts. The extension of the cuts to the edges of the card opens out the pop-up to create a form which is particularly sculptural and very unlike a typical 'greetings card' pop-up. The pattern of backward-facing and forward-facing 'V's could be repeated several more times if the card was taller. Like all Piercing the Plane constructions, it also looks good when seen from the back.

4.     RELEASING
       THE FOLDED
       EDGE

**4.3    Piercing the
       Plane**

4.3.3  No Wings

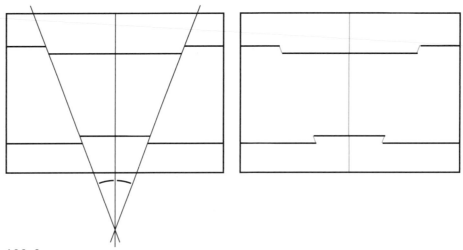

**4.3.3 _ 2**
The non-parallel folds seen above in 3.4.2
on page 56 can be adapted to the Piercing
the Plane technique. As in 4.3.3 _ 1, the
cuts to the left and right edges of the card
can be placed in any of the four positions
seen in 4.3.2 _ 2 and 4.3.2 _ 3.

The effect of the converging folds is to create a pleasing non-vertical central feature, similar in appearance to an open book. It is equally effective when seen from the back, though the 'book' is now seen from the back. Whichever way around the pop-up is seen, this simple converging technique creates dynamic and interesting forms.

### 4.3.4 Asymmetrical Piercings

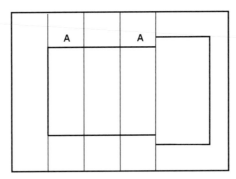

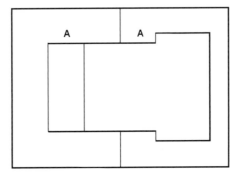

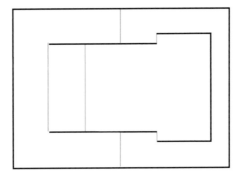

**4.3.4 _ 1**
Piercing the Plane need not be done
symmetrically. It can also be done
asymmetrically, using the 'Asymmetric
Pop-up' techniques described in 2.3
on pages 33–39 as the basis for the
placement of the folds. Examples can
be made with or without the wing
cuts, described on previous spreads
in this section.

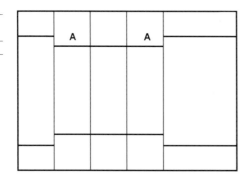

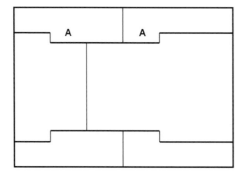

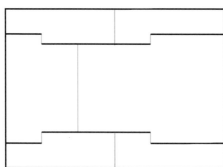

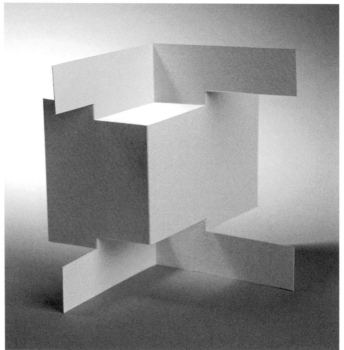

**4.3.4 _ 2**
The wings example shown opposite can be made so that the cuts extend to the left and right edges of the card, to create an asymmetrical variation of 4.3.3 _ 1.

4.      RELEASING
        THE FOLDED
        EDGE

**4.3     Piercing the
        Plane**

4.3.4   Asymmetrical
        Piercings

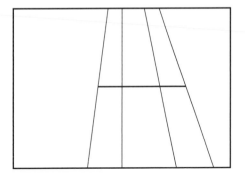

**4.3.4 _ 3**
This is the construction seen previously
on pages 58–59, which describes how to
make Asymmetrical Converging Folds.
It will be used again here to make an
Asymmetrical Piercing pop-up, with
asymmetrical angles.

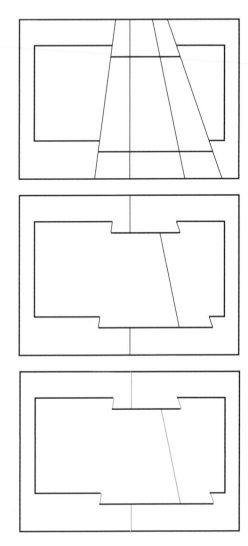

**4.3.4 _ 4**
Remove the single cut across the middle
of 4.3.4 _ 3 and substitute it with four
separate cuts, as shown, in the manner
of a Piercing the Plane construction.
Remove the excess lines in the manner
of the construction described on pages
58–60, mentioned in the previous
caption.  The result is shown in the
photograph opposite.

The effect of the asymmetrical angles
piercing is an apparent distortion of
perspective that can be unsettling. It
may also be made without the wing cuts,
thus liberating the off-centre pop-up
form from its confining frame. Although
relatively complex to construct, this is
a pop-up technique that is well worth
exploring in detail, as it can create
forms and planar effects that are
very unorthodox.

# 05:

## MULTIPLE GUTTERS AND GENERATIONS

## Introduction

This chapter shows how to make multiple gutters and multiple generations. The effect of these relatively advanced techniques is to produce pop-ups with numerous intricate facets, which explode the surface of the card into many intricately related fragments. It is also the chapter that completes the set of primary techniques needed to understand how a flat sheet of card can be transformed into a pop-up. There are, of course, many other techniques but they become increasingly complex and esoteric, and perhaps also decreasingly relevant to a pop-up created to hold surface graphics.

This is the most technical of all the chapters and must be read with care. Be sure to make many of the examples and, along the way, be prepared to sometimes feel a little unsure of where you are going or how you achieved what you somehow just completed. It often helps to make notes on what you are making, both to help you understand the next step, but also to act as an *aide-mémoire* for the next time you use the technique. If you ever get stuck, just collapse shut the pop-up you are making and see what happens to the folds and cuts. You may not make exactly what is in the book, but if what you made has flattened, you have made a pop-up!

## 5.1 Multiple Gutters

So far in the book, all the pop-up constructions have been built from just one gutter crease. However, it is possible to increase the number of gutters from one to any number and by doing so, make the pop-up forms increasingly complex.

### 5.1.1 Two Gutters

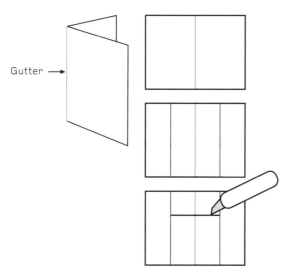

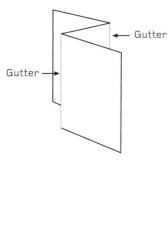

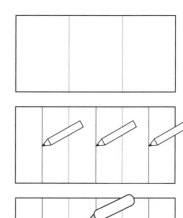

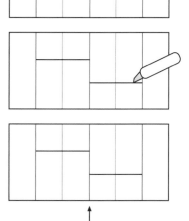

**5.1.1 _ 1**
To recap, this is the cut-and-fold pattern used previously in the book. The gutter is the crease down the centre. It is flanked by two vertical lines drawn on the quarters and these lines are connected by a horizontal cut.

**5.1.1 _ 2**
With two gutters, one is a mountain fold and the other is a valley fold. In this example, the card is seen stretched widthways compared to 5.1.1 _ 1 and the gutters are placed to divide the card into thirds. Drawn lines divide the card into sixths. The first cut is placed across the mountain gutter, in imitation of 5.1.1 _ 1. A second cut crosses the valley gutter. Crucially, both cuts begin or end on the vertical line drawn between the gutters. That drawn line is common to both gutters.

This line is common
to both gutters

5.   MULTIPLE
     GUTTERS AND
     GENERATIONS

**5.1   Multiple**
      **Gutters**

5.1.1  Two Gutters

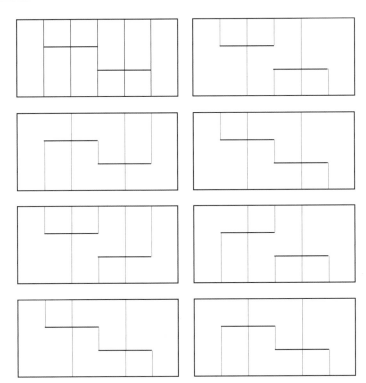

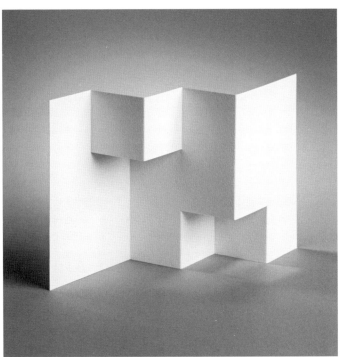

**5.1.1 _ 3**
Here are the seven possible 'Three and
One' and 'Two and Two' crease patterns
for the drawing made in the previous
step (reproduced again at the top left of
this step). Sometimes, the two pop-ups
made on the two gutters seem to exist
independently of each other, whereas at
other times they appear connected by
a short fold which links the two cuts.
It is well worth making these seven
examples to study carefully their
similarities and differences.

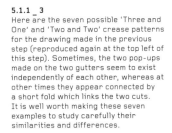

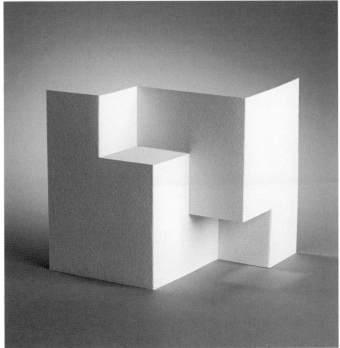

5.    MULTIPLE
      GUTTERS AND
      GENERATIONS
**5.1   Multiple**
      **Gutters**
5.1.1  Two Gutters

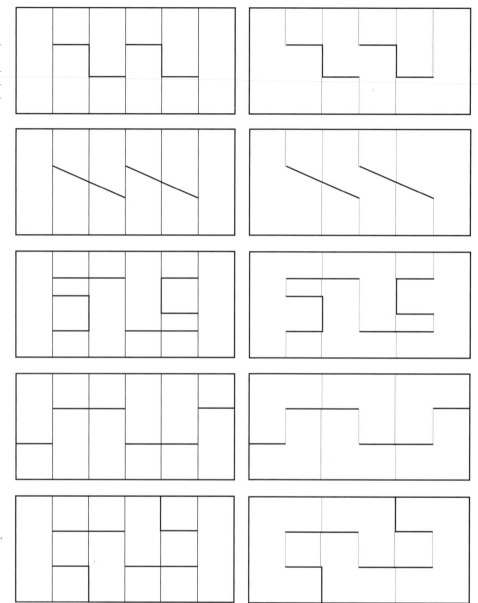

**5.1.1 _ 4**
Here are five further examples, using different
techniques learnt previously in the book. For each
drawing shown in the left-hand column, there are many
variations. Just one variation is shown in the right-hand
column. Although still relatively simple, these examples
which use only two gutters display a pleasing complexity
of form.

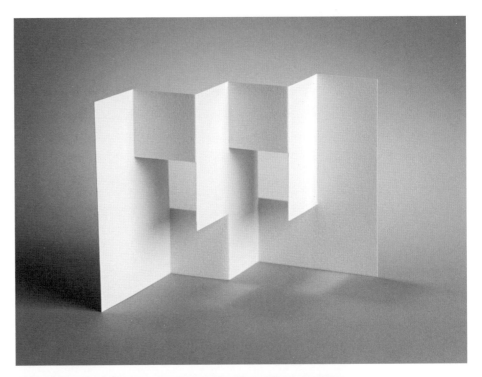

These two pop-ups are the
top and bottom examples
illustrated opposite.

### 5.1.2 More than Two Gutters

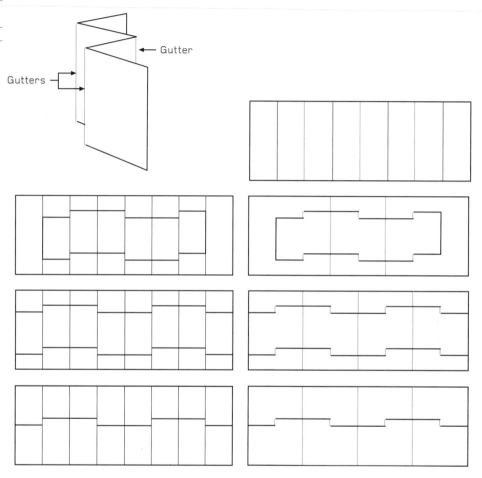

**5.1.2 _ 1**
This example shows three gutters. Note
how the gutters alternate mountain/
valley/mountain. A longer sequence of
gutters would continue this alternating
pattern. Note too how the cuts are
connected by short creases. The three
examples shown here are just a few of the
numerous cut-and-fold possibilities using
the 'Three and One' and 'Two and Two'
crease patterns.

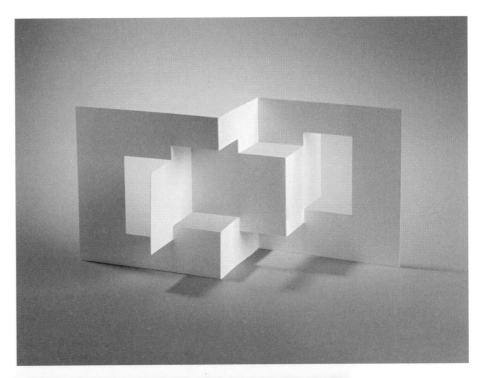

These two pop-ups are the
top and middle examples
illustrated opposite.

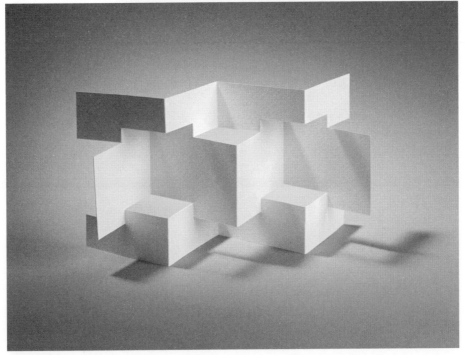

5.    MULTIPLE
      GUTTERS AND
      GENERATIONS
5.1   **Multiple**
      **Gutters**
5.1.2 More than
      Two Gutters

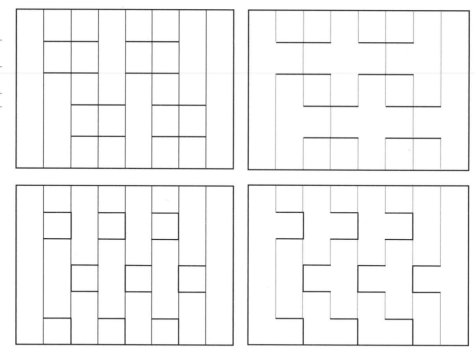

**5.1.2 _ 2**
Finally, two sequences of seven gutters,
which divide the card into vertical
eighths. As before, the gutters alternate
mountain/valley/mountain/valley... With
an ever-increasing number of gutters,
the card becomes ever more corrugated,
and features a large number of facets
suitable for complex layouts of surface
graphics. One caution though: these
complex sequences of zig-zag gutters are
narrow and susceptible to falling over in
even the faintest breeze. One solution is
shown in the lower example, where the
bottom edge is broken into just four long
'feet' that stand with more stability than
the eight-part zig-zag shown in the
upper example.

## 5.2 Generations

To close the book, a section which is relatively technical, but which, if you have read much of what has gone before and worked through it with diligence, will be quickly assimilated. An understanding of how successive generations of pop-ups can be created and linked together will increase your technical vocabulary more than any other section in the book.

### 5.2.1 A Theory of Generations

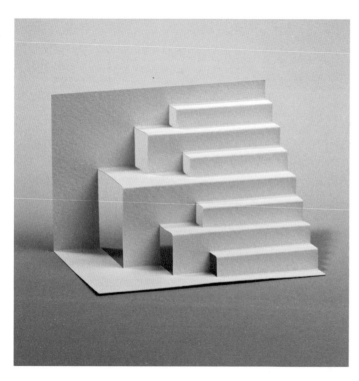

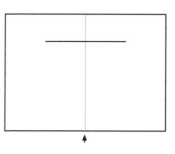

New gutters

**5.2.1 _ 1**
Any pop-up is a combination of two basic elements: a vertical gutter crease and a cut which crosses the gutter (see 2.1, on page 24).

**5.2.1 _ 2**
Further vertical creases in either the 'Three and One' or the 'Two and Two' pattern will allow the pop-up to 'pop' into three-dimensions. Shown here is a 'Three and One' pattern. These new creases can in turn be used as gutters to create two second-generation pop-ups...

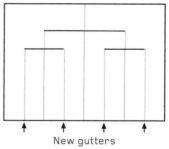

New gutters

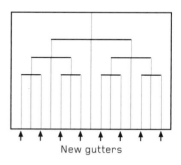

New gutters

**5.2.1 _ 3**
... like this. Note how two new cuts have been made. Each of the two new pop-ups has created two new creases, which means that four new gutters have been created. These new creases can be used as gutters to create four third-generation pop-ups...

**5.2.1 _ 4**
... like this. Note how four new cuts have been made. Each of the four new pop-ups has created two new creases, which means that potentially eight new gutters have been created on which eight new pop-ups could be made... and so on down successive generations. Of course, not every potential gutter needs to be used and the symmetrical structure seen here could become very asymmetrical.

The primary pop-up is built on one gutter. When completed, that pop-up will have created two new folds, which can in turn be used as gutters to create two second-generation pop-ups, which when completed, will create four new creases, which can in turn be used as gutters to create four new pop-ups, which when completed will create eight new creases, which can in turn be used as gutters to create eight new pop-ups, and so on. The number of potential pop-ups doubles at each generation (1, 2, 4, 8, 16, for example). Pop-ups do not need to be built on every new crease. This means that many asymmetrical patterns can be created, not just the one, full, symmetrical set.

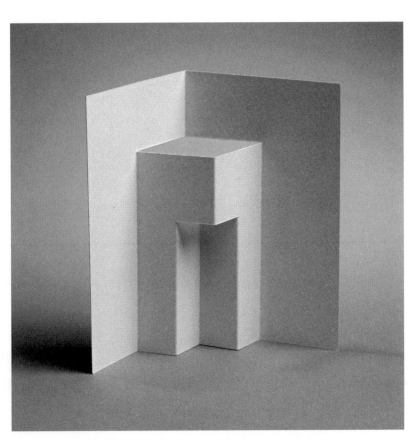

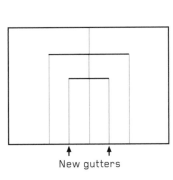

New gutters

**5.2.1 _ 5**
It is also possible to nest generations to build successive generations on the original central gutter crease. Each generation need only be slightly smaller than the one preceding, enabling many generations to be created on just the one gutter.

## 5.2.2 Two Generations

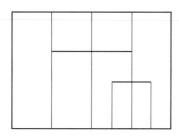

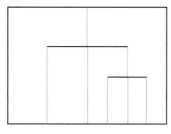

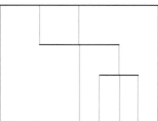

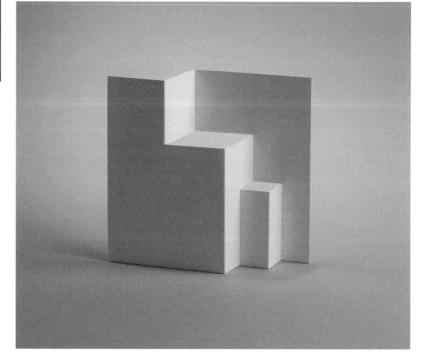

**5.2.2 _ 1**
The top illustration shows a drawing for
a first-generation (primary) pop-up and
a second-generation pop-up at the lower
right. The middle drawing shows the
first generation folded as a 'Three and
One' pop-up, whereas the lower drawing
shows it as a 'Two and Two' pop-up. The
second-generation pop-up is the same
in both examples. In many instances,
pop-ups with two or more generations
can use either folding pattern.

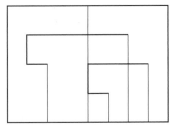

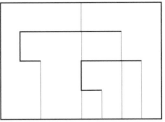

**5.2.2 _ 2**
This is similar to 5.2.2 _ 1, but shows
how both generations of the pop-up
can be opened out to create a more
faceted effect.

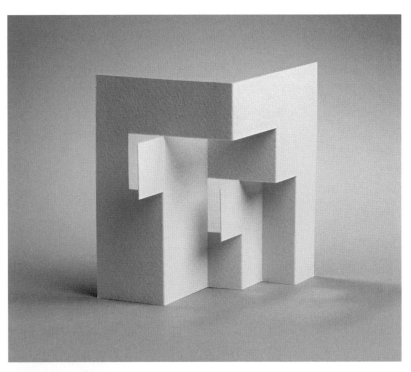

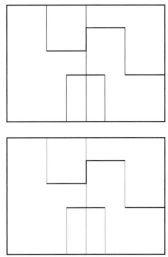

**5.2.2 _ 3**
The two pop-ups are not first and second
generation similar to 5.2.1 _ 5 above, but
exist independently of each other. For
this reason, they may be regarded as
co-existing first-generation pop-ups.

### 5.2.3 Asymmetrical Generations

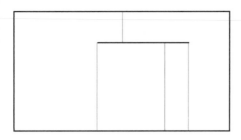

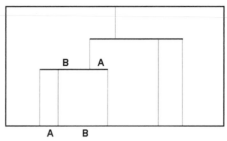

**5.2.3 _ 1**
This is a typical first-generation
Asymmetrical Pop-up, described in 2.3,
page 33. The left-hand fold will be used
as the gutter for a second-generation
asymmetrical pop-up.

**5.2.3 _ 2**
This is the completed second-generation
pop-up. The method of construction
is exactly the same as for the first
generation: A = A and B = B. Several
generations of asymmetrical pop-ups can
be constructed, creating structures of
great complexity.

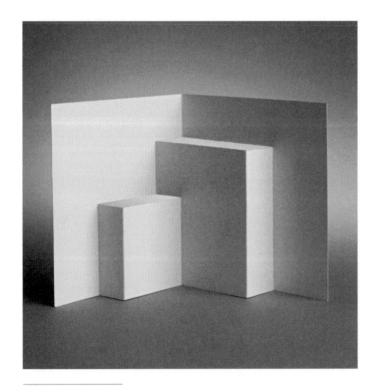

### 5.2.4 Asymmetrical Angle Generations

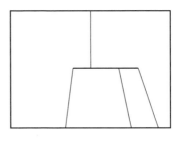

**5.2.4 _ 1**
This is the drawing for a typical
Converging Folds: Asymmetrical Pop-up,
described above in 3.4.3 on page 58. The
left-hand fold will be used as the gutter
for a similar second-generation pop-up.

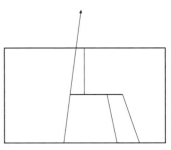

**5.2.4 _ 2**
First, extend the left-hand line.

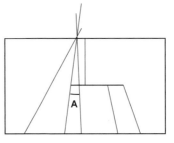

**5.2.4 _ 3**
Draw two new lines which converge on
the extended line. Note that angle A is
smaller than the angle to its left.

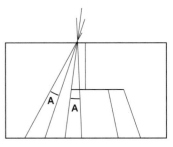

**5.2.4 _ 4**
Measure angle A and draw a new line of
the same angle. A = A.

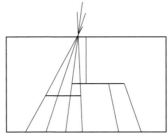

**5.2.4 _ 5**
Draw a horizontal line to connect the
vertical lines.

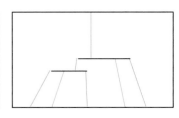

**5.2.4 _ 6**
Erase all the unwanted lines, cut and
fold the card as shown. The result
is a strangely disorientating pop-up
with a distorted perspective. Further
generations may be added.

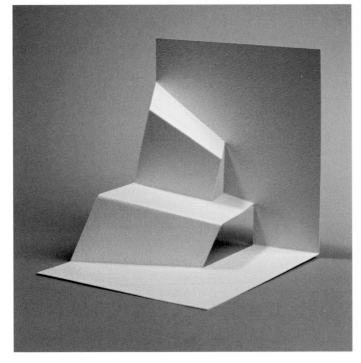

### 5.2.5 Opposing Generations

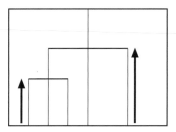

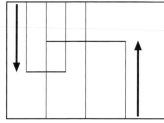

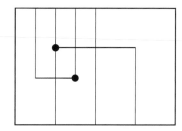

**5.2.5 _ 1**
This is the structure of the first- and second-generation pop-ups described above. Both pop-ups rise upwards from the bottom edge of the card.

**5.2.5 _ 2**
By contrast, this structure has the first generation rising from the bottom edge, but the second generation is descending from the top edge. They are opposing. The method for resolving the pop-up structure of these opposing generations is relatively complex and must be followed precisely.

**5.2.5 _ 3**
When fully drawn, the two horizontal lines (the cuts) terminate at the two circles. These circles need to lie on the same vertical line. Thus, at present, the drawing is incorrect.

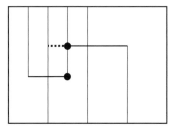

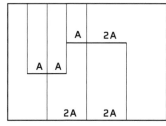

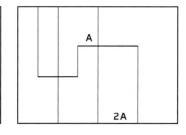

**5.2.5 _ 4**
The method to correct the drawing is to terminate the first-generation cut on the same vertical line (the crease line) as the second-generation cut. The two circles are now on the same line. The dotted line shows which section of the first generation cut is to be erased.

**5.2.5 _ 5**
This is the new drawing. Note the equal distances A and 2A (2 x A). However, the drawing needs further correction.

**5.2.5 _ 6**
Removing part of the first-generation cut in step 4 has created the distance A on one side of the gutter and 2A on the other side. Clearly, the two sides of the pop-up are now unequal and this first-generation pop-up is currently problematic. It will not 'pop' into three-dimensions and then flatten.

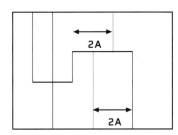

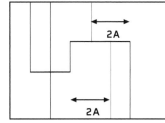

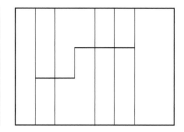

**5.2.5 _ 7**
One solution is to move the top section
of the gutter to the right, so that 2A =
2A. This is now a standard asymmetrical
pop-up, described in detail in 2.3 (see
page 33).

**5.2.5 _ 8**
The alternative solution is to move the
lower part of the gutter to the right, so
that 2A = 2A. Either of the two solutions
will work.

**5.2.5 _ 9**
Finally, this is the fully corrected
drawing. The five long lines will be used
in different combinations to create many
different pop-ups, as described below.
Note that the only short crease connects
the two cuts.

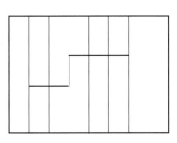

**A**

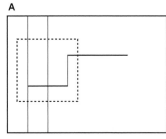

**B**

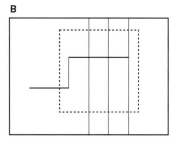

**5.2.5 _ 10**
The drawing divides into three parts.
The first part is the short crease that
connects the two cuts.

**5.2.5 _ 11**
The second part (A) is the pop-up
structure on the left, including the
short crease.

**5.2.5 _ 12**
The third part (B) is the pop-up structure
on the right, including the short crease.

**5.2.5 _ 13**

There are two ways to create A as a pop-up: the top left-hand drawing shows a 'Three and One' crease pattern and at the top right, a 'Two and Two' pattern. Both drawings include a short valley fold that connects the cuts. These are the only two possible crease patterns for A.

However, there are four possible crease patterns for B, shown in the bottom four drawings. Either of the two A patterns can be combined with any of the four B patterns, to make a total of eight possible pop-up structures if a short valley fold connects the two cuts.

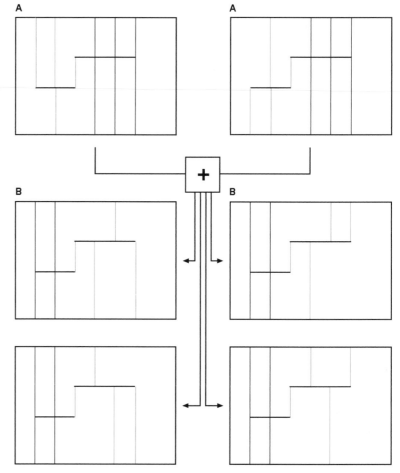

These are two of the
eight possible A + B
combinations, illustrated
opposite.

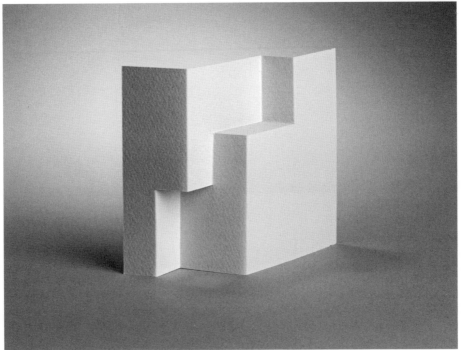

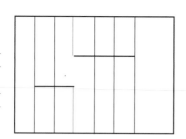

A

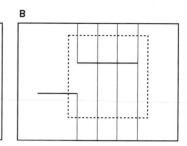

B

**5.2.5 _ 14**
A completely different set of eight pop-up structures can be created if the short valley fold that connects the two cuts is eliminated and replaced by two folds (one a valley, one a mountain) which extend to the top and bottom edges of the card. These two folds are the first of three parts to the pop-up.

**5.2.5 _ 15**
The second part (A) is the pop-up structure on the left, including the two creases discussed in the previous step.

**5.2.5 _ 16**
The third part (B) is the pop-up structure on the right, including the two creases discussed in the previous step.

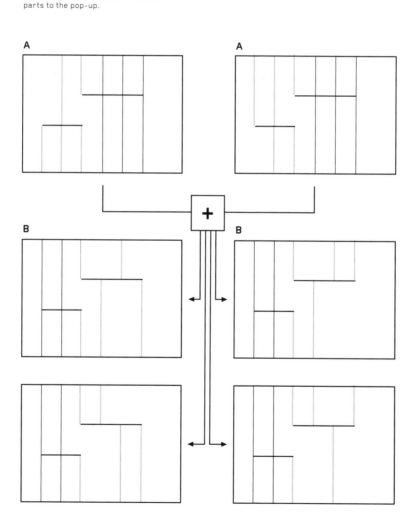

**5.2.5 _ 17**
There are two ways to create A as a pop-up: the top left-hand drawing shows a 'Three and One' crease pattern and at the top right, a 'Two and Two' pattern. Both drawings include the two short folds that connect the cuts to the top and bottom edges of the card. These are the only two possible crease patterns for A. However, there are four possible crease patterns for B, shown in the bottom four drawings. Either of the two A patterns can be put with any of the four B patterns, to make a total of eight possible pop-up structures if two short folds connect the cuts to the top and bottom edges of the card.

Remarkably, when this step and step 13 are combined, there are 16 possible pop-ups that can be made using just two simple cuts. When these simple cuts are replaced by more complex cuts, the creative possibilities become almost endless.

These are two of the eight possible A + B combinations, illustrated opposite.

## Create Your Own Pop-ups

Here are some suggestions (in no particular order) to help you connect between working from the book and designing your own pop-ups.

### 1 Have You Read the Book?

For several years in the mid-noughties, I taught a course on Paper Engineering to Degree students of Graphic Communication Design, for half a day a week for a semester. Three or four of the lessons were about pop-ups. Anxious to cram in as much knowledge as possible, I overreached and taught too many complex pop-up techniques, skipping quickly over the basics. The students complained that they didn't understand much and I was asked by the head of the course to please not teach pop-ups again! However, unbeknownst to him, I taught pop-ups the following year. Having learnt (I hoped) from my mistakes, I spent my allotted time teaching only very simple techniques – nothing advanced – followed by a quick creative project at the end. The work made by the students was wonderful! Suddenly they were confident and creative and showed that they had clearly learnt the basics well. The more adventurous found Origami Architecture books and began to absorb and use the complex ideas they contained.

In its content and pace, this book is based on that course (and on subsequent courses in other colleges). I'm confident that if you have read the book with a degree of diligence and have made many of the examples it contains, you will be able to create innumerable designs of your own.

So, I ask again: have you read the book? As with all things, the more you put in, the more you get back. You can't expect to be The Next Great Pop-up Artist if you've only flicked casually through the pages. Effort is always well rewarded.

### 2 Make Heroic Failures

An ex-student of the pop-up designer Vic Duppa-Whyte once told me that his mentor would advise his class that if they couldn't see how to make a 3-D multi-piece model of something fold down flat, to first build it, then to squash it flat (!), analyse how it flattened and reconstruct it accordingly, incorporating the folds and cuts made when it was flattened! It may sound brutal, but the method essentially works.

Similarly, with one-piece pop-ups, don't think too much; instead, make too much. Cut and fold the card quickly, perhaps without measuring anything, and keep squashing it flat to see how it reacts. If you have made an unnecessary cut, heal it with a length of sticky tape rather than start afresh with a new sheet, taking a fresh sheet only when the current sheet is wrecked beyond use. If you need an extra cut, make it; if you need to move the folds, move them.

With this sense of creative freedom, you will find many new forms that will collapse flat. Of course, much of what you make will be less than useful – these are the Heroic Failures – but the looseness and speed of the process will enable you to design pop-ups of great originality. Nobody needs to see the failures and you need not be embarrassed by them – they are a vital part of developing a great piece of work. Failure is an essential part of the creative process: the more you fail, the more you'll succeed.

Also, because card is quick to cut and fold, and inexpensive, you'll not be spending significant amounts of time and money developing creative threads that might lead nowhere. Be bold, be brave, work quickly and take risks. It's just a bit of card.

## 3 Combine Techniques

There simply isn't enough space in the book to show how all the different one-piece pop-up techniques it describes can be combined in different ways.

Here then, is an incomplete list of 'put this with that', to set you thinking how technical themes can work together.

| | | |
|---|---|---|
| Piercing the Plane | PLUS | Asymmetrical Pop-ups |
| Piercing the Plane | PLUS | Asymmetrical 'V' Folds |
| Asymmetrical Pop-ups | PLUS | Generations |
| Multiple Gutters | PLUS | The Shape of the Card |

... and so on. It is, of course, quite possible to combine three or more ideas together, though the more elaborate the combinations become, the more like a doodle a design can look. Complexity for its own sake is rarely successful, in pop-ups, as in any area of design.

## 4 Keep It Simple

Creating one-piece pop-ups is a design game defined by its rules (only one sheet of card may be cut and folded and it must fold flat). Rather like origami, or even openings in chess or bidding in bridge, one-piece pop-ups offer endless labyrinthine variations which may be pursued endlessly for little practical gain, but which can give great intellectual satisfaction in the pursuit. It is relatively simple – and very seductive – to repeat a cut-and-fold idea across a sheet of card, to create complex corrugated surfaces of great beauty, but of questionable practical use if the pop-up is to be combined with a printed surface.

The ideal is to find a pop-up idea that is simple and subtle, but which still showcases the printed surface and which still has a big 'wow' factor. If the pop-up takes attention away from the printing, the overall design is out of balance.

So, explore the labyrinth of variations if you choose, but remember... the good news is that technical virtuosity is not necessarily an advantage when it comes to designing a one-piece pop-up which features a printed surface.

CREATE YOUR
OWN POP-UPS
**How to Produce
a Pop-up**
1    By Hand
2    By Computer

## How to Produce a Pop-up

There are three different ways to produce a pop-up:

### 1. By Hand

This is the simplest, most direct and most low-tech way to make a pop-up, but also the most labour-intensive. If you are making only a very few, or even a one-off, then it can be the preferred method.

In our household, we make many one-off pop-ups for clients and also for family birthdays and anniversaries. Our off-the-peg repertoire doesn't usually need to extend much beyond intriguing abstract forms and the usual cheesy hearts or birthday numerals, though we try to present them differently each time. We cut these motifs from the card as a pop-up, or cut the edge of the card to the silhouette of the motif, or simply draw the motif by hand with coloured pens on a flat expanse of card. If we want to incorporate a longer greeting or message, we usually write it on the computer, print it out and glue it on. The same process is used for printing out photographs and gluing them onto a pop-up.

These cards are typically made quickly at the last minute but, despite the haste, are always well received and are guaranteed to make someone feel extra-special.

### 2. By Computer

Computers and computer printers are an excellent way to make low-production runs. With vector software a pop-up structure is easy to design accurately and graphic software can create any printed surface you can imagine. It's a matter of temperament how many you can print and then cut and fold by hand, before wishing you had never started. If your patience is limited, keep the assembly as simple as possible.

For a top-quality finish, a professional digital printing company can print your designs, though at a cost.

CREATE YOUR
OWN POP-UPS

**How to Produce
a Pop-up**

3    By
     Manufacturing

## 3 By Manufacturing

This will be a three- or four-way production between you, an offset printing company, a die-cutting company and possibly also a graphic designer to prepare the graphic files for printing. No hand process can quite match the satisfying precision of work made by machine.

Manufacturing is, of course, the only sensible way to create large numbers of pop-ups, but also the most complex, the slowest and the most expensive. If you are creating a pop-up for a client, be sure you have the budget and the time before committing yourself to anything.

An alternative to die-cutting is to laser cut. This can be very expensive per unit, but offers the possibility of cutting remarkable filigree-like detail, which die cutting can never achieve.

A further cut-and-fold manufacturing option is to purchase a special cutter made for home and office use which looks and operates much like a regular computer printer, but which instead of printing, cuts and scores lines with a special knife. I know professional and semi-professional designers and paper artists who use them regularly and who create great work with them, while others regard them merely as a novelty. If you regularly need professional-looking results in low numbers and don't trust your hand skills, a programmable cutter/creaser is well worth your consideration.

## Acknowledgements

I had the privilege to twice work with the late Professor Masahiro Chatani —
the popularizer of Origamic Architecture — and must thank him for introducing
me to the spectacular world of one-piece pop-ups. I must also thank Paul
Johnson for his inspiration for using pop-ups both as an educational tool
and as an art form, and the Movable Book Society for its important work
documenting and contextualizing the history of pop-ups.

Most of all, I must thank students of design on many courses in several
countries, who over three decades unknowingly road-tested many of my
teaching ideas, until I came to more-or-less understand which pop-up
techniques could be generally taught, understood and used creatively.
Without you, this book could not have been imagined or written.